MW01234487

Endorsements

I found Mike's writing to be very insightful into the world of addiction. His honest chronicling of his faith journey and his battle speaks deeply to those engaged in a similar struggle. I particularly appreciated how he let his story flow from narrative to poetry. I personally thought the most powerful part of the book was in the description of the event where he was able to save his nephew. That's a very moving story.

—Rev. Clay Smith
Sr. Pastor Alice Drive Baptist Church
Sumter, SC

Don't miss Michael's story. Don't resolve to read about his life and come to a conclusion and miss the Father. Don't miss the Holy Spirit that was speaking and still speaks. God gave to Michael a gift in meeting people and loving them, and also to paint, write, and express himself in vivid detail. He took the time all along his journey to tell you what was going on, but also "Who" was helping and living within him.

You can read this and possibly find yourself identifying in some ways with Michael. Make sure you don't miss HIS voice as He speaks through Michael's life and experiences. HIS voice still speaks today. Do you care to hear? Don't miss HIM!! That's why Michael used his gifting.

—**Rev. Ken Oates**
Assoc Pastor West Rome Baptist Church
Rome, GA

We came to know Michael—his life story and his struggles—through our relationship with his parents at our church. He was a truly unique person, a warrior for God and an unabashed advocate for the saving power of Jesus Christ. Mike was unafraid, in any circumstance, to seek out those who were most in need of God's grace and present that message in a language only they could understand. He was especially suited for this task because of his own battle with addiction, his personal relationship with Jesus, his knowledge of Scripture, and his abiding love for people. At his funeral we heard many testimonies from those whose lives were completely changed when the Lord arranged for them to meet Mike. We pray that these writings will inspire those imprisoned by the demons of addiction to see that ALL things are possible to those who truly seek His grace and forgiveness.

—**Dave & Jean Wall**
Rome, GA

PRISON
VISION

AN ADDICT'S

VISIONS WHILE

IN PRISION

MIKE WATERS

WinePressPublishing
Great Books, Defined.

Unless otherwise noted, all Scriptures are taken from the *Holy Bible, New International Version*®, *NIV*®. Copyright © 1973, 1978, 1984 by Biblica, Inc.™ Used by permission of Zondervan. All rights reserved worldwide. www.zondervan.com

Scripture references marked LIVING BIBLE are taken from *The Living Bible*, © 1971 owned by assignment by Illinois Regional Bank N.A. (as trustee). Used by permission of Tyndale House Publishers, Inc., Wheaton, Illinois 60189. All rights reserved.

Scripture references marked NEW KING JAMES are taken from the *New King James Version*. Copyright © 1982 by Thomas Nelson, Inc. Used by permission. All rights reserved.

ISBN 13: 978-1-4141-2299-1
ISBN 10: 1-4141-2299-3
Library of Congress Catalog Card Number: 2012901024

PSALMS 91:1 (Living Bible)

"HE WHO DWELLS IN THE SHELTER OF THE

MOST HIGH WILL REST IN THE

SHADOW OF THE ALMIGHTY"

Dedications, Special Thanks, Honorable Mentions

FIRST AND FOREMOST: This book is dedicated to Jesus Christ, Lord of Lords, King of Kings, and my personal Savior. I am nothing without you, Jesus, and I thank you.

SECONDLY: With sincere appreciation, I'd like to thank my mom & dad for their undying love and support. You two never gave up on me or cast me out. You loved me when I didn't love myself and stood in the gap for my soul's defense.

THIRD: I'd like to raise a praise to the Apostles Ron & Hope Carpenter, Jr., and give a shout to Minstrels Sam & Paula Shelton of Redemption World Outreach Center. "Can't be explained, only experienced."

FOURTH: My "Doodle." There aren't enough ways to say, "I'm sorry," but I am sorry.

FIFTH: With honor I'd like to acknowledge Kay Wilfong who always told me: "Anything worth doing is worth writing down." Well Kay, I've finally been given something worth doing!

SIXTH: Allen Chambers. You were my best friend. You had a contrite heart and a willing spirit. I'm sorry I couldn't recognize your pain. I wish that you had stuck it out.

HEAVENLY SEVENTHLY: The Holy Spirit of God Almighty as given by the life, death, and resurrection of Jesus Christ. It has quickened this mortal body to life exceedingly, abundantly above all I ever imagined!!

Lloyd Michael Waters was born on September 5, 1966, in Weisbaden, Germany, to US Air Force Tech/Sgt Lloyd S. and Barbara Waters. He had a sister, Amy Jo, who was 4. He attended schools in Hawaii, Florida, Ohio, and South Carolina. He graduated from Hillcrest High School in Sumter, SC. He had many friends, played football, and excelled in baseball. He graduated from the University of South Carolina with a degree in PE.

Drugs came into his life in high school, starting with marijuana. By college it was all sorts of hallucinates and others. His best friend, Allen, (story on page 125) committed suicide while they were in college and that began Mike's addiction to opiates.

Mike started with the Methadone clinic about eight years ago in hopes of satisfying his need for opiates. They drug tested him weekly, charged him $10.00 a day (which kept his expenses down a great deal), and it seemed to help him stay away from "street drugs." We both knew that he was trading one drug for another, but Methadone seemed safer and cheaper. He went to help with the disaster in New Orleans from Hurricane Katrina and was able to find a clinic there … had to get up at 4:00 AM and drive an hour, but he did it every day!! After a couple of years, the desire to get high from other things came back and he sought out crack and "benzos." These are drugs that you should NEVER use with Methadone. This is eventually what overdosed Mike.

Mike accepted Christ into his heart at the age of 18 and never broke that faith, no matter what situation he found himself in. He always praised God and led many people to see the goodness to be found in believing in Jesus. We miss him, but know exactly where he is and that he is safe in Jesus' arms. There will come a day when we will see him again.

Mike was married three times, but each ended in divorce because of his addiction. He led all three of his wives to the Lord and saw each one of them baptized in the name of Jesus.

As Jesus asked the Father to "take this cup from me, yet not my will, but Your will be done" (Matthew 26:39), I know that Mike prayed for God to take his cup of addiction from him too. But God had other plans.

His life, though short and ending tragically, was all to the Glory of God!!

Philippians 1:12 (New King James)
"But I want you to know, brethren, that the things which happened to me have actually turned out for the furtherance of the gospel."

CONTENTS

Georgia, Floyd County Jail –
May 2008 – September 2008

Bainbridge, Georgia, Drug Rehab Program –
October 2008 – March 2009

INTRODUCTION
"THE CHARGE"

Most prison inmates do their best to avoid receiving an extra "charge" that could result in additional time or punishment. This is usually best accomplished by sidestepping conflict, maintaining a "low profile," and, above all else, keeping your mouth shut! Sounds simple enough, but despite my best efforts to incorporate these basic techniques into my daily walk, I still found a way to "volunteer" for extra duty. On the morning of May 14, 2005, I found myself "caught in the mix" and the following "charge" was issued:

"**The word of the Lord came to me:** Son of man, speak to your countrymen and say to them: "When I bring the sword against a land, and the people of the land choose one of their men and make him their watchman, and he sees the sword coming against the land and blows the trumpet to warn the people, then if anyone hears the trumpet but does not take warning and the sword takes his life, his blood will be on his own head. If he had taken warning, he would have saved himself. Since he heard the sound of the trumpet but did not take warning, his blood will be on his own head. If he had taken warning he would have saved himself. But if the watchman sees the sword coming and does not blow the trumpet to warn the people and the sword comes and takes the life of one of them, that man will be taken away because of his sin, but I will hold the watchman accountable for his blood."

"Son of man, I have made you a watchman for the house of Israel; so hear the word I speak and give them warning from me." Ezekiel 33:1-7 (LIVING BIBLE)

So you see, this book is that warning against the army of the Enemy. I have to write these words as instructed by the Holy Spirit of God Almighty. Whether you read them or not isn't the only objective. I have to "sound" the alarm first; what action is taken next is not up to me. If I refuse to warn the people, their blood is upon me. God has allowed me to be an eyewitness to His miraculous grace and mercy, as well as to the depravity and despair associated with the Enemy. My life has been preserved and protected for the preparation of His appointment as "watchman." I humbly and gladly accept this "charge" and therefore sound the alarm. My only concern is that I do so with enough vigor and clarity for you to hear it!!

"There is no three ways about it!" This book is designed to accomplish two objectives. The first is to illustrate and demonstrate the very real power of God's love and mercy. The second is to unveil the hidden forces of darkness and the plots they construct while attempting to destroy our lives. You may find these words to be entertaining or even humorous at times. They may lead you into deep thought or retrospect, or they might even cause you to cry and mourn. Whichever the case proves to be, let it be known that the events depicted between the covers are true to the fact without additions or subtractions. All the "near misses," the "could haves," the "should haves," the "would haves," and the "almosts" are real events that will point to God's grace and redemptive power.

These are episodes of good vs. evil, positive vs. negative, destruction vs. deliverance, light vs. darkness, beauty for ashes, and dancing in exchange for mourning. It is Jesus against Satan and Satan against Jesus and the internal struggle within us all. It will ask the question: "What on earth are you doing for heaven's sake?" It will state: "Get right or get left." It will guide you in the directions of God, "turn right, and stay straight." The best result will inspire and encourage you to pursue Jesus with a passion and confidence in Him. The worst result will leave you in doubt and disbelief. I encourage you to relax your defenses and open your imagination as these words do their best to take you to these times and places where God's hand can actually be seen. Some names have been changed to protect the guilty. But, aside from that, these are true-life stories, near death experiences, and poetic letters from "home."

May God bless you for the time you invest and faith you employ.

Mike Waters

THE BOOK

This is how the book should go
I'm writing it down so in the future I'll know.
Just about how and what it should be
A helpful guide for setting people free.
I'll explain right from the start
That it's wisdom I wish to impart.
A journey through my life's experiences and trials,
About the chemistry set I had that's now nothing but
    empty beakers and broken vials.

It will state quite clearly all its intent
With random samplings, short stories and poems I've
    penned.
I'll take the reader by the hand,
Gently leading them to the Promised Land.
Trying my best to explain and show.
Freely giving away all that I know.
My aim and attempt will clearly be,
Loosing the prisoners, helping the blind to see.

PRISON VISION

In between my poems and tales,
I'll do my best to part the veils,
The curtains that block the sun coming in.
Right from the rip is where I'll begin,
Hopefully just one soul will be saved
And given the chance to walk anew down the road that
    I've paved.

SOUTH CAROLINA
STATE PRISON–
MARCH 2005 – MAY 2005

My Last Day Before
My Last Day

*Mike had been in Columbia, SC, State Prison for 3 months and was due to be released the next day when he received this poem from the Lord.

How I want to praise you Lord, this day before my
    last.
Time creeping slowly, is now running fast.
That day You came and stole me; I knew not what lay
    ahead.
The day I was arrested and snatched from my bed.
Police car I was stuffed, hands behind my back, cuffed.
It was Your plan to save me, put me on Your track.
The Kingdom is taken by violence; I see it clear as glass.
I needed Your power and might to rescue me at last.
Questioning the logic behind Your hidden plan,
Pain was my enemy from which for many years I ran.
You also knew this would convince me beyond a shadow
    of doubt: the road was a rough one, struggles far
    from few.
Kicking and screaming and pulling my hair, what else
    could I do?

PRISON VISION

Was it the drugs or demons making me feel this way?
Thrown into prison, a place I didn't want to stay.
It was Your arms stretched around me, disguised as
many fences.
Your love began pursuing me, the chase it was relentless.
Taken from the game I wasn't winning, there was little
I could do.
Looking down, You saw the frown engraved upon my
heart.
You brought me here to make it clear—I needed a
brand new start.

But more than that, You had in mind for me to win
this race.
A test of me, this entire time, to take me to Your secret
place.
As I kept livin', Your word was given, planting a seed
of hope.
I'd thought the only way to get "high" was from
constantly taking dope.
Your Spirit came by exposing that lie and showing me
the "ropes."
All the desire to continue in sin now was answered
"nope."
You gave me a chance to find the "Most High."
The rush was enormous, I swear I don't lie.
What happened to me early day, I think around 6 AM,
Touched me in a special way, I'll never be the same again.

MY LAST DAY BEFORE
MY LAST DAY

It turned my insides out and darkness into light.

Making all that had been wrong suddenly switch to
right.

I laughed, I cried, it couldn't be denied—something
was going on.

Shouting and praising hallelujah, would it last long?
Last it has, in fact it has even grown.

You took the plan the Devil had in his hand, snatched
it, tore it in two.

Filling me with Your Holy Spirit, You've made me
completely brand new.

Showing me the way, that beautiful day, You told "who,"
"what," and "how"—Saying without hesitation, "I
want you to start now.

"Write these things, which I've let you know,

Write them down for yourself and all the world to show.

You have this gift for spirits to lift; accept it with gladness and joy.

Tread on serpents and snakes, demons' necks you'll
break, powers of darkness destroy.

I've brought you thus far, no matter where you are, I'll
always be right there.

Take up your cross and follow Me.

Mount with eagle's wings, fly way up in the air.

Keep Me in your secret place and of you, I'll always
take care.

PRISON VISION

Remember, my son, it's just only begun, so be sure to
take your time.
Don't try and do this in your own strength, I want it
done in Mine.
I'll be there, through my Spirit to lead and to guide.
Listen for My voice and hear it, do not leave My side,
Let My love push your pencil, don't resist and let it be.
Keep your feet firm on the ground.
Reach out to My lost, I want them to be found.
Let the poems and stories be not about you,
Explain the strength of My power and all that it can do.
Share just how far I'm willing to go,
To keep My children from dying, they need to know.
Describe all the times you should have been dead.
Reveal all the destruction that "whizzed" past your head.
Contrast and compare the hate of the Devil and the
love of My core.
Give clear examples that prove your hairs are numbered
And the way I watched over you, even while you
slumbered.
More than you, tell them of Me.
The suffering and pain I endured on Calvary.
The nails in My hands, the pierce in My side,
The crown of thorns and the tears that I cried.
Laughed at and rejected, spat in My face.
All this I let happen to save My human race.
I made them and loved them, wanting them to be
with Me.

My Last Day Before
My Last Day

I let Myself be crucified to take them back from the
Enemy.
I endured the cross to recapture that which was lost
And make a way where there was none.
That's why, just before I died, out loud I cried 'It is
done!'"

Satan laughed and cheered, but beneath this veneer the
battle had been won.
Jesus went into the ground, where he was found and
stripped him of power and might.
Now he sneaks around, scared to make a sound, usually
hiding at night.
He's the one to blame for bringing the sin and shame
into this world of mine.
So tell the stories and those poems, I think it's about
time.
I had to walk through that Valley of Death so everyone
would know,
Those words I'll be writing are true—not just for show.

"So rejoice my son, the work has begun, as evidenced
on this page.
I am the Alpha and Omega, always will be from now
until the end of the age.
Don't forget to stop and pray, asking for My help.
I'll be there to assist you as on your knees you're knelt.

Have some fun, bask in the Son, and enjoy the warmth
    He brings.

Put Me first, go to church and I'll give you everything.

Stay in at night, always act right and I'll keep you safe
    and sound.

I let you get so lost, in order for you to be so found.

Worry no more, I've evened the score, in fact we're way
    ahead.

Live this life without struggle or strife, for now My son,
    you're no longer dead!"

HOW LONG?

How long can this go on? It almost feels wrong,
To write and write and write.
Just when I've finished one, comes another.
Is there no end in sight?
I might as well, if I'm stuck in jail, with little else to do.
The only way it can be O.K., let it not be all about me,
But rather You.

Let me tell the true story of how You were born one
night.
Born in a barn, way out on a farm, with very few in
sight.
It was Your plan to be disguised as a man, wearing a
suit of flesh,
Living a perfect life, despite all the strife.
You passed that cruel test.
People called You a fool, tested Your cool and accused
You of many things.
"Surely He's not the Prince of Peace, where's His robe,
see any rings?"
Never dismayed or easily swayed, Your mission You
knew well.

7

PRISON VISION

Coming to heal and set free all those in need, You came
to keep us from hell.

Explaining Your ways through endless nights and days,
the labor must have been hard.

One touch from Your Spirit will free the heart that
hears it, no matter how badly scarred.

I know this to be, for it happened to me, it's why I'm
writing this page.

As mentioned before, if you're keeping score, it's all I
can do at this point and stage.

So, allow me to continue, if you will, there's so much
more to say,

I mean write; rather, it's been happening all day.

On and on it comes to me in phrases like nickels and
dimes,

Not sure where it's going or how it will even rhyme.

But somehow it does, here lately more often than just
time-to-time.

The style of writing is not what's exciting, it's the One
written about.

I've got the indescribable urge that I need to purge, or
stand on a mountain and shout.

For, if it wasn't for Him, I'd be dead in my sin and life
would make no sense.

I'd probably be sitting here whining and counting my
time in here behind this fence.

HOW LONG?

Instead I'm enjoying each word He's employing with
    endless combinations and riffs.
Hope you're not snoring or finding it boring, I need
    you to catch my "drift."
This isn't being written, no matter how smitten you
    may seem to be
For more entertainment or a lesson from life or even
    history.
The crux of the matter lies straight away,
It's in these words given as His Spirit tells me what to say.

Shall we return to the one who was "burned" with lies
    and false witness?
I'm sure it's best we do that now and do it with
    quickness.
Of Jesus I'm writing with gladness in my heart,
He'll show me how to end this; He showed me where
    to start!

Let's discuss a miracle He did, the one He did for the
    first time.
That's right, if you're paying attention, He turned water
    into wine.
Not just any wine, but one of a special kind, the best
    ever tasted.
It was so good, to all that around stood, and not a drop
    of it was wasted.

9

PRISON VISION

Only a pinch of the power He had, His time He'd
    rather spend making sad hearts glad.
That's what He did for me one day; He lent me His
    Spirit, now it's here to stay.

So I'm writing and writing about His miraculous touch,
It's all I ever needed, and wanted so much.
I plan to wear out this pencil explaining everything to
    you,
Writing and erasing, it's all I know to do.
For more than time just passing, I've got to get a
    message through.
A message of love and sacrifice done all for you.
Jesus has the power of created life inside.
His light exposes darkness, it has no place to hide.
If your soul has a frown, just sit right down, consider
    these words sincere.
He can take a broken life and turn it around, expelling
    all doubt and fear.

Put your trust in Jesus, you must for He's the only way.
Don't stop to think or allow eyes to blink; do it now
    without delay.
Christ is the One to get the job done; He's done it
    many times before,
Just ask the blind man or the cripple who sprang up
    from the floor.

H O W   L O N G ?

Listen to all the things He said, the people He fed, the
    time He walked on water.
Consider the seizure boy calmly returning to his father.
Maybe try Lazarus fresh from the tomb,
How 'bout the supernatural conception inside Mary's
    womb?

If all these things won't let freedom ring, then maybe
    His suffering and loss.
The way He let Himself die, nailed to a cross.
"Forgive them," He kept pleading while His wounded
    back was bleeding.
"They know not what they do."
He kept His mouth silent enduring the beating.
He did this for me and you.
The curses that were said, crown of thorns upon His
    head,
The sign that read "King of the Jews"
Can you really deny Him? Can you actually refuse?

What if all this pain and torture "ain't" your cup of tea?
What if His brutal death and hurried burial doesn't
    make you see?
Let's move on to the next part of this rambling text.
Move on to the best part of all, the part that happened
    next!
You see Jesus was more than just a man martyred on a
    cross,

He was God Almighty in the flesh, with power in His
veins to save the sinner lost.
He had to die like that, no other way to choose.
He took our sin upon His back,
So He could pay all of our dues.
The debt was paid, but no way would have been made,
if in the grave He had stayed.
After 3 days of stompin' the Devil, the door on His
tomb He did level,
And emerge alive and well.
I know it's true, that's why I'm writing to you,
For in my heart He has come to dwell.

Resurrection power has quickened my bones, canceling
all my loans, way overdue.
He's done it this way, don't run now, just stay, and read
a little more.
You might feel someone knocking, maybe even
pounding on your heart's door.
It must be Him so let Him in; you won't be sad or sorry.
He'll lift that weight, cast it aside with all of your worry.
Only Jesus can do this miracle inside,
Exposing the works of darkness,
Leaving them no place to hide.
For this reason above all, He took the scourging and
allowed Himself to die.
But as I've mentioned before, you may even recall,
He is the "Most High," "Lord of Lords," and "King of
Kings."

HOW LONG?

His Spirit will leave you no doubt,
One touch from my Savior you'll have to run and shout.

So if you've been thinking that Jesus might be for you,
The next parts you'll be reading will tell you what to do.
Just come to God pleading as humbly as you can,
Asking for salvation according to His plan.
The one that Jesus fulfilled in the heights,
The one that's designed for you without any bias.
Admit that you're a sinner in need of all His love,
Admit that He is risen, no longer in the grave, but
    rather up above.
Denounce the works of Satan, instead accept His love.
By His Spirit He'll rush to be at your side,
By His Spirit He'll come to you and make you feel alive.

I would not tell you this had it not been true for me,
But it's simple and fast,
For I was blind, but now I clearly see.
I know it can happen for you if He was willing to do
    it for me.
You have to decide, it can't be denied.
So what's it gonna be?

Will you stay locked in your cage or will you go free?
I've done my best; He'll do the rest.
I think I'll stop writing and go play some chess!!

SITTIN' AND THINKIN'

Sometimes I just sit and I think about the things that
   I've done.
'Bout all the games that were played, that I've lost and
   I've won.
Never understanding, or even givin' a thought,
'Bout the pain I was causin' the Blood of the Lamb.
I was just runnin' and chasin' and makin' a mess.
Thinkin' I was broken even though I was blessed.
Tired of the struggle which had taken me down.
Given' into evil, always wearin' a frown.
Fightin' and swimming and tryin' my best,
It didn't seem to matter 'til I was under arrest.
Then all the pain I had caused was put back on me.
Behind all the walls full of bars, fists clenched with
   rage, with agony.
Until the One that I knew stepped in on a prayer,
Began lifting me up, way up in the air.
Lookin' down from His grip, I had the chance to see,
I wasn't defeated or beat or needin' set free.
What I was needin' the most, had already been done,
It was in the Father, the Holy Ghost, and His only Son!!

FREE BIRD

Isaiah 40:31 (TLB)
"But they that wait upon the Lord shall renew their
strength. They shall mount up with wings like eagles;
they shall run and not be weary; they shall walk and
not faint."

I woke up this morning with you on my mind,
There's something I need to tell you, so I'm droppin'
    you a line.
I wanted you to know I think you're really cool.
A gentle, pure spirit, you ain't nobody's fool.
You've got many gifts inside you and you rock at
    basketball.
That could be what I tell you, but trust me, that's not all.

While here in prison nobody goes by name, rather
    where you're from
Or how you look is what usually brings the fame.
I hadn't been called by anything other than my name,
Until that day you "tagged" me, I haven't been the same,
You see, I've been locked in a cage of guilt and shame
    for time too long to tell.

15

PRISON VISION

I've lived with demons' torment, straight from the pits
of hell.
Not even knowing this to be my case,
I kept my chin up anyway while struggling in this race.
My secret name was "failure," the "tag" I had come to
know.
I had lost my sense of victory from all the many
blows.

But God had a new name He wanted me to get.
He used you to give it to me, that's why I know it's
legit.
Our paths crossed one day; I thought there'd be no
word.
I nodded and smiled; you looked back and simply said
"Free Bird."
I didn't feel free in any shape or form,
But God names His children way before they're born.

A few weeks later I was covered with His Spirit,
Covered so profoundly I could actually hear it.
"You are no longer caged." I know I heard Him say.
"You are a Free Bird from now on, go fly away."
I've taken to the skies, soaring with delight.
The things that kept me bound are nowhere in sight.

FREE BIRD

So I wanted you to know, God had used you in a
   special way
To give me my new name on that special day.
I'm thanking you sincerely from the bottom of my
   heart.
Thanking you for helping me make my new start.
Now my prayers are turned toward you,
That you continue to seek God, so He can touch you
   too.
I'm sure that you know Him; I can see it in your eyes.
Just keep your guard up from Satan and all his feeble
   lies.
I pray He continues to use you in many special ways,
Like the way He spoke through you on that special
   day.
That's really all I wanted to tell you,
I've given you the word I wanted to tell you.

Good-bye for now.
Your friend,
Free Bird

PEACE IN THE VALLEY

Well, there is Peace in the Valley, brighter than the
morning sun.

It came to me on the 14th of May in 2005.

Took me back to where it begun.

It came into me; I didn't even try to run.

The love of the Father, the Holy Ghost, and His Son.

It took me deep, deeper than the ocean floor.

Now my pain and my sorrow won't be bothering me
any more.

'Cause His light put out the darkness that kept me
bound for so long.

Kept me bound, so bound, couldn't do right only wrong.

But now I'm free, freer than the birds above.

Full of joy, full of peace, full of His redeeming love.

I thought I could never feel this way.

Especially when I took a look at my past full of sin and
despair everyday.

But He did it, He really did it, and that is what I'm
here to say.

Now there's peace in the valley, brighter than the
morning sun.

PEACE IN THE VALLEY

It happened on the 14th of May, took me back to where
He begun.

Now I know why His people are so happy despite what
might be in their way.
It's 'cause we've been given keys to the grave, no longer
in we have to stay.
For my ashes, He gave me beauty, turned them right
before my eyes.
He took my mourning and gave me joy. I promise now,
I tell no lies.
So now I'm a witness to the Power of His touch.
He died for you and He died for me. He died because
of love so much.
Just take His hand, let Him lead you. You don't have to
run this race.
Let His Holy Spirit come inside you, take you to that
secret place.
You'll be oh so glad that you did it, I told you I
wouldn't lie.
There'll be peace in your valley as you dwell with the
Most High.

HERE HE COMES

Here comes the Son, Lord, and Savior.
He's come to me, to show me favor.
Now I'm in love, love, love with the Son.
He is my King, full of Power.
He let freedom ring at the appointed hour.
Now I can stand up and shout without a trace of doubt
"Here He Comes!"

The marvelous light shines from His eyes,
The world can't relate, they would rather despise.
Love without bounds, seeking the lost 'til they have
    been found.
So just hang on, it won't be long.
"Here He Comes!"

With power and might, He'll win the fight,
For the battle is not your own.
Have no fear, at His time of year,
Life will spring from the seed sown..
Bursting inside, darkness will hide,
Love will conquer the hate.

HERE HE COMES

The time is now, come, run quickly, hurry, and don't
    be late.
"Here He Comes!"

Do your part, prepare you heart,
It's all you need to do.
Get ready, make yourself steady,
For He's done it all for you.
His train will fill the temple; it's really quite simple....
"Here He Comes!"

DINNER WITH
THE DEVIL

Luke 4:3 (TLB)
Satan said, "If you are God's Son, tell this stone to become a loaf of bread."

Chow had all but been consumed from the plate.
Perched at the table with two others, sitting in silence,
  we ate.
I had no idea of the company with me,
Merely chewing on my food, washing it down with tea.
A question was raised, suddenly catching my ear.
I offered the answer, felt no reason to fear.
"What is meekness?" one fellow pondered.
Drawing my focus from where it had wandered.
"Meekness is strength under control." I responded with
  free offering.
He seemed to really want to know, I didn't suspect a
  thing.
Jesus on the cross was the illustration I used.
Praying for those who hurt Him even while being
  abused.
He could have come down from that cross and done
  something about His fate.

He could have come down at any time and done something great.
They seemed to nod in agreement at the picture that
was drawn,
They seemed to be friends, not enemies, in my mind it
never dawned.

"That's very interesting." they claimed back at me.
"You should stop by our room to share some more;
we're in cell 1103."
Thinking not much of it at the time,
A trap was being set which later I would find.
An hour or so had passed since leaving the hall,
I nearly forgot the whole conversation, nearly forgot
it all.
That's when I found the Scripture from God's Holy
Word.
I should go and show it to them, will they think it
absurd?

With eagerness to share something I had been shown,
I entered the room with Satan himself, who would have
ever known?
The two men who ate dinner with me,
Faces lit up upon my entrance, smiling with glee.
Saying there was more I'd like to share,
"I'll read it to you, if you don't care."
Words from Revelation were read out loud,

PRISON VISION

They said I had done well, said they were proud.
That's when I noticed something was askew,
My spirit felt oppressed and I wondered what to do.
Questions were being asked by both of them at once,
Too many questions to answer, making me feel like a
dunce.

Beginning to wonder where all this was headed,
My soul gave me the answer, the one I had dreaded.
They seemed to be using the truth as a way of telling
me lies.
No light was shinning—only darkness when I looked
deep into their eyes.
Suddenly I knew what to do, be patient and stand my
ground.
Answering their questions with "I don't know" as they
circled around.
The barrage grew stronger and more and more intense.
Acting as though persuaded, I put up little defense.
Again I gazed into their eyes,
Seeing the Prince of Darkness, despite this clever
disguise.
They tried to tell me at one point that Jesus wasn't
really God.
I let them think me convinced, as I gave them a
confused nod.
Onward they went with pages turning and Scriptures
bent.

DINNER WITH THE DEVIL

One on my left side, one directly to my right.
They seemed to know everything and could have gone
    on all night.

That's when my spirit said, "Enough, exercise your
    clout."
Putting my hands together like a referee, I called "Time
    out!"
Both of them were blabbing, trying to speak as one,
When the signal that I gave them, let 'em know they
    were done.
With boldness and clarity, I spoke without parody and
    set them in their place.
"I know the foul spirit at work here and I can see it in
    your face.
Don't try to tell me that Jesus was not God,
Don't think I was convinced even though my head did
    nod.
I'm full of His Holy Spirit and I see the evil in you,
I don't want to be mean, but what you gonna do?

"Because since day one the Devil has denied the Son
    and tried to exalt himself.
His ugly spirit used to be in me until he was placed on
    a shelf.
So if you will excuse me please,
I need to be alone and pray on my knees.

25

Thanking God for showing me the trap you tried to spring.

Thanking Him that all your lies didn't mean a thing.

But one last question before I go,

With all your understanding and knowledge, what was it you wanted to know?

Something about meekness, I'm sure it's true,

Did you think I would fall for it? Is that what you thought I would do?

Well, your trap has been shut with a snap and I'm walking across this floor.

I still love you though in the name of Jesus,

But don't ever come around me with that mess no more!"

CONCRETE AND STEEL

Concrete and steel, make it difficult to feel
The world passing us by.
We sit, we stand, and we
    hold our heads in
    hand,
Finding no reason to lie.

The lock tumbles shut,
The keys jingle and fade
    away,
The door remains closed.
Silence is imposed
Until tomorrow begins another day.
Down for the night,
Watching the fade of light,
We hope and we pray,
Waiting for the Day all will be right.

IF

If lies were diamonds, I'd own a jewelry store.

If tears were feathers, I'd fly away.

If pain were pleasure, I'd want more.

If I got what I deserve, I'd be here to stay.

If six were nine, you'd be mine.

If eight were great, I wouldn't hesitate.

If time were well spent, I'd have the rent.

If love were a dove, it would come from above.

If words were water, we would walk on farther and
  farther.

If hope was dope, there' be none.

If you were me, there'd be no need to worry.

If joy were jam, I'd spread it all over the land.

If up were down, we'd never frown.

If I could sing, my head wouldn't zing!

If air were a stare, I'd be there.

If water was wine, I'd be drunk like swine.

If boredom were a flower, I'd be a garden.

If I were President, I'd receive a pardon.

If concrete were gold, I'd be living in Fort Knox.

If beige were clear, I'd walk right out of here.

If nervousness were peace, I'd have that at least.

If return meant send, I'd be at … The End!!

SLEEP?

I've been waiting for this moment for weeks.

Do "they" honestly expect me to be able to sleep??

This can't be the case, at this stage of the race, I really beg to differ.

If there were anything I could do, I'd surely do it, making this time pass swifter.

For now I'll spend my time coming up with rhymes and scribbling them on this page.

Other options I may have include reading or beating on the door with rage.

But I'm not mad; I'm actually quite glad—nearly to the point of tears.

It's only been a few months or so, but feels like it's been years.

The reason for that, I could surely explain,

If you'd like to continue, jump aboard this train.

I've got nowhere to go and plenty to show, just don't cry or complain.

If reading in rhymes drives you out of your mind, maybe stop right now.

I could probably share my thoughts some other way, but I'm not really sure how!

So climb aboard, strap yourself in,
Where it will stop is where it begins.

Back to front and front to back, I'll share it all, nothing
will lack.
I want to tell of my freedom found here in this cell, so
remind me to stay on track.
The point I'll make is that I didn't have to wait for
release to be set free.
For one day a couple of weeks ago, the Holy Spirit
came in here and fell right on me.
It put an end to a long, sad story of struggle, pain, and
grief.
It washed away all my trouble; it came as quite a relief.
I had no idea this would happen that day,
I was simply reading my Bible and getting ready to
pray.
A thought came to mind how I might spend some time
indulged in a newfound text.
Maybe I should wait to complete my prayers, I wasn't
done just yet.
Waited I did, putting a lid on my can of worms called
prayer.
I sent them off in the name of Jesus. Sent them off in
the air.

SLEEP?

A moment or two had passed—remembering finally at
    last,
The magazine waiting for me.
I pulled back my mat and there it lay flat, a little jagged
    around the edges.
Presenting itself as a garden of sorts, I eagerly dove into
    its hedges.
What to read? My eyes danced just shy of light speed—
    absorbing color and detail
Flipping the pages, I found an article—read this one—
    might as well.
It began to explain, like clear skies absent of rain, stories
    of death and survival.
Of people who died but still were alive as a result of
    their revival.
While away they all had something to say including
    God and Jesus,
Those two mentioned in a *Rolling Stone* mag? I could
    hardly believe this.
Continuing on, it soon began to dawn—this was no
    coincidence.
The details and similarities I found dispelled all my
    feelings of indifference.
Reason why? You know I won't lie about things of
    which I write.
For the truth shall set you free and bring an end to your
    entire plight.

So let me continue to try and try, being clever and
   creative, using all my might.
To tell this story with details so gory it'll keep you up
   at night.

Where was I, can you help me?
Something about being in prison yet feeling so free?
Ah yes, allow me to digress and pick up where I left
   off.
Jesus in a *Rolling Stone,* I nearly choked and coughed.
Reading on as words lay before me, my mind was
   blowing,
For I witnessed the same exact story.
The tale of a child who fell deep to the bottom of a pool.
They experienced the horror so bitter, so cruel.
They were found dead, no life signs in head or even
   body for that matter.
They seemed to be gone, climbing those steps long,
   ascending on heaven's ladder.
God held their hand and enacted His plan sparing us
   from such loss.
He let me know for sure, that He alone is Boss.
Both were revived, to this day they're alive and well
That's what makes this worth writing about and sharing
   like show and tell.

My own nephew, Chad, was the one who had drowned
   and sank to the bottom.

SLEEP?

It happened on a day in the middle of summer, not
 spring, not autumn.
My dad was the one, once the rescue began, to dive in
 and fetch him.
After he came out we all stood in doubt, should we
 squeeze him or stretch him?
I said a quick prayer deep in my spirit,
"Please God listen. I need You to hear it.
What should I do and how should I do it?
Make it clear, dispel all of my fear—just whatever, let's
 get to it!"
I fell to my knees, Chad's little nose I did squeeze, while
 pulling open his chin.
He needs air, needs it badly; start blowing
 quickly—begin.
Nothing at first happened, my spirit began to doubt.
I could hear his dad praying and saying "No!" with a
 shout.
Just when it seemed Chad would be lost,
Jesus stepped in and said, "Remember, I'm the Boss!
Now give him some air, use your mouth to put it in
 there and get right to it.
This child I'll spare with tender care, don't hesitate, just
 do it."
That's when the miracle of life did fall,
It came right down bestowing us all with wonder and
 amazement.
Chad gasped for a breath, cheating this death,

We all clung to hope and gave God praises.

Making a long story short, he went on to play sports
and bear fruit from the Spirit.
One day in time, if you don't mind, I'll explain the rest
if you really want to hear it.
Get comfy, take a deep breath, there's more I still need
to say.
Back to the mag, in which I had found this true-life
story.
The details inscribed on the pages inside hit me so hard,
it floored me.
Just like Chad—this tale started bad and didn't seem
hopeful in the least.
But this was a girl who drowns, somebody's daughter,
somebody's niece.
Dead on arrival, major efforts for revival fell short of
realistic chances of survival.
Prayer was induced, the family reduced to tears and
bended knee.
That's when Jesus showed up, said "Drink from my
cup, for I am He."
She came back to life right there that night, right before
her family.
Now this is enough to write all this stuff, it stands alone
on merit.
If nothing else had happened, I'd still want to share it.

This is the part that pounded my heart and gave the
    adrenalin rush,
Flooding my eyes with tears and turning my soul to
    mush.
Both Chad and this girl were escorted to a world where
    Jesus and His Father did dwell.
It's the reason He didn't leave them, He needed them to
    return with a story of love to tell.
These two children while seemingly gone away from us,
Could explain every detail from the ordeal without
    hesitation, without fuss.
No one had told them or had time to hold them when
    events they did divulge.
Things from the bottom of the pool, where stomachs
    full of water caused their tummies to bulge.
They knew who, how, and why; saw people who cried,
    and remember talking with Jesus.
They were simply stating the facts—words weren't
    spoken in order to please us.

All this I read while propped on my bed, jaw dropping
    with every word.
The story was clearly intriguing, finding it in a *Rolling
    Stone* completely absurd.
It went on to say where she is today and all else she told.
Somebody wrote a book about it, 13 million copies
    were sold.

That's when the bubble did burst, it wasn't rehearsed,
    and I careened out of control.
I felt the Holy Spirit, like a wind I could hear it, touch
    and tickle my soul.
It changed me forever and plunged me into the deep.
All this in my mind so cleverly rolling over and over….
And "they" expect me to sleep??

DROWNING POOL

Sometime during my early teenage years, my parents managed to have an in-ground swimming pool installed in the back yard. Instant popularity soon followed as many of my peers jockeyed for after school invitations to swim and sunbathe. Summers were an endless splash fest from sun up to sometimes well into the night. Whether with friends, or equally as often by myself, the pool was the center of my existence throughout my junior and high school life. I was responsible for the upkeep and took great pride in its cleanliness and clarity. Even in the winter I still had to keep watch over the pool by making sure too many leaves didn't accumulate on the cover. Over the years, I spent countless hours either in or around the pool, but little did I know that it would be the site for one of the most dramatic events of my life.

Chad was my sister's first child. He was the first grandchild in our immediate family and was cause for celebration. The entire family had come together at my parents' house for a reunion of sorts, and the pool was the center of our activities. Chad garnered most of the attention, as the summer sun only outshined his bright personality. He was only two years old at the time, but already had quite the vocabulary for a child his age. As we lounged on the deck and splashed in the pool, he would courageously jump from the sides into the outstretched arms of his grandparents and other family members. He was becoming quite the little aqua-man, able to hold his breath with each dunking and come up all smiles.

I was playing a game of "stick ball" with my cousin in the yard adjacent to the pool. I remember hearing the random squeals and cheers that went up every so often as Chad made the rounds from person to person. He was in paradise, the same oasis of refreshment that I had come to know via the pool. As the late morning activities neared high noon, a lunchtime break was in order and it wasn't long before I heard the call for chow. Everybody filed into the house from every direction—cousins from the back porch, aunts and uncles from the pool, and me from the yard. "A quick bite to eat and we'll finish our game," I assured my cousin.

The kitchen and adjoining dining room became a collage of swim suit clad relatives, glistening with tanning oil, faces streaked with fading sun block and funny oversized hats. The smell of barbecued chicken permeated the air and there were visions of potato salad and cantaloupe wedges. The hunger from a morning filled with swimming and sunning had left everyone in a "fend-for-yourself" mentality, evident from the hurried positioning taking place around the table where the food was displayed. I joined the fray and made sure to get myself a sufficient amount of everything before it got gone! With plates bending from the variety of food, everyone spread out to find a place to sit momentarily. Iced tea was held delicately between the knees by those who hadn't found a spot at the table and a hush took over the scene as talking gave way to chewing.

My thoughts were elsewhere; I was there in body, but I can't really say what my mind was focused on. I think I just wanted to get back to my game of "stick ball" and enjoy the rest of the day. I definitely wasn't concerned about Chad; there were plenty of people watching after him and looking back on it now, I'd say that he might have been the last thing on my mind. But that was all about to change and it changed in a hurry! As I nibbled away the last bit of chicken from the bone, I heard someone ask a question that nobody wanted to answer. "Where's Chad?" I'm not sure who said it first, but before long everyone was asking it. With so many people there, I figured Chad would be found soon enough and didn't take it upon myself to look very hard for him. I remember seeing my family slowly growing concerned and darting off in different directions while simultaneously calling "Chad!"

My cousin had picked up the bat and ball and called for me to join him back in the yard to restart our game like I had promised. As I exited the back porch, I glanced over my left shoulder toward the pool, taking notice that the water was flat calm and nothing seemed out of place. My dad was walking right beside its edge, but must have been focused on the gate, which led to the front of the house. He called out for Chad while striding around the pool and out the gate. Somehow I took this as no sign for alarm and began to put my full attention into the "stick ball" game. No sooner had my cousin stepped up to the plate and I was winding up to deliver a pitch, when I saw something that will live in my mind forever.

Just like in a special effects scene, I saw my dad coming back through the gate by the pool and, as if in slow motion and sound, with a look of sheer horror on his face, he yelled, "Oh-God!!" Before I could process just what was happening, I saw him leap headlong into the pool, even though he was fully clothed. I knew instantly what was happening—that question that nobody could answer, the "Where's Chad?" question—well, Dad had found him and he found him on the bottom of the pool. He had been there the entire time. When lunch was called, Chad had doubled back to the pool while everyone else focused on eating. My family is not irresponsible, but this was just one of those times when everyone thought someone else was watching Chad. I can't blame anyone because I was just as guilty of thinking the same thing. Like I said before, my mind was elsewhere and finding Chad was someone else's job. But all that changed in the blink of an eye. I can still picture my dad frozen in time, suspended in midair, fully dressed, shoes and all, look of terror on his face, impatiently waiting for gravity to pull him into the water.

Now, I must have been a good 40 yards or so from the pool, but I have no recollection of myself running in that direction. I literally jumped time and found myself at the pool's edge just as my father was pushing off the bottom and thrusting Chad through the surface and into my arms. Before I had a moment to even think, I was there with Chad's lifeless and blue body in my arms. His eyes were rolled back in his head and by every account he appeared to be dead. A rush of adrenaline surged through my body as my mind raced with thoughts of what to do. Mike, my brother-in-law and Chad's father, was there next. He was in full panic mode and grabbed Chad by the feet, shaking them up and down while saying "God-no, oh-God-no" My peripheral vision noticed the rest of the family around us and the clamor of chaos ensued. I had taken a CPR class a year before in preparation for a lifeguarding job at the Air Base nearby, but this was no simulation, it was too real to comprehend and time was of the essence. Time seemed to stand still but I could hear it ticking by like a freight train. Mike continued to cry, "Oh God no, please, please, no!" while he hurriedly turned Chad over and pushed on his back. Water gushed from his mouth and nose as if he were a large sponge that had just been retrieved from a bucket. Another push on his back and more water flowed seemingly from every orifice on Chad's body. I was still trying to decide what to do, how to do it, and where to start. The clamor around me was turning into tears and I remember saying a quick prayer:

"God help me, tell me what to do."
"I'm scared Lord. I need you now!"

I said this while trying to listen for a heartbeat, all the while Mike continued to shake Chad's legs and beg God. That is when I heard the Lord say "AIR-get him some AIR! And do it now." I motioned for Mike to stop and give me some room. He complied by letting go of Chad and giving me full control. I pinched Chad's tiny nose and pressed my mouth against his blue lips, noticing his lifeless eyes still rolled back in his head. I breathed into his mouth and instantly more water gushed into my face with the smell of vomit and chlorine. Normally this would have sickened me, but this was Chad and love crosses all barriers. I didn't even flinch. I turned his head to the side and let the rest flow out. Once it stopped, I repositioned his head, pinched his little nose again and gave him another breath. As soon as I administered this second attempt, Chad's diaphragm sparked to life and he drew in a breath just like someone after having the wind knocked out of them. It was a guttural suction sound, followed by some coughing and a little more vomit water. I gave him another breath and he began to cry faintly. Color returned to his lips, but his eyes were still full of unconscious evidence.

While all this was taking place, my Uncle Kenny had the foresight to jump in his van and was arriving around back, through the yard. With perfect timing, the doors flew open and Mike scooped Chad up and we both jumped in the van, whisking Chad away to the nearest hospital. Shaw Air Force Base was only 10 miles away and was the nearest Emergency Room available. I barked directions from the back while Uncle Kenny drove like a bat out of hell. Chad was unconscious, but still faintly crying. Mike and I poked and shook him in an attempt to aggravate him into crying harder. My mother and sister stayed behind momentarily in order to call the Base hospital to expect our arrival. Again, time seemed to stand still, even though Uncle Kenny was passing every car we happened upon with the precision of a NASCAR® superstar. Once we made it to the gated entrance of the Base, all protocol was abandoned and the usual routine of saluting the guard and waiting for him to approve our access was replaced with a shout out the window and a hand gesture that said, "We're in a hurry!" I saw the guard shack blur past through the window along with the bewildered soldier.

"Keep going!" I commanded, "the hospital is down this road on the right." Chad was wheezing and coughing in a congested cry. I thought about continuing mouth to mouth, but decided against it since he was breathing well enough to cry. Mike continued to pray. "God, please don't take my son." I wasn't cognizant of it at the time, but I'm sure the rest of the family, still at home, was circled in prayer also. Looking back on it now, I'm sure I was in a state of shock. I wasn't panicking; it was all so sublime, like a dream. I was numb.

Before I knew it, the Base hospital made its appearance through the van windows. "Right here." I barked at Uncle Kenny as he whipped into the parking lot in front of the ER. I was expecting to see white coat clad doctors and a gurney awaiting us, but to my dismay, the entrance was desolate and nobody seemed to be ready for anything. Regardless of this, Mike grabbed Chad, cradling him across his chest and burst into the ER as I held the door. "Surely," I thought, "there will be people ready to jump into action and help save Chad's life." You know, like on TV. But contrary to my expectations, only one doctor was attending to Chad once we laid him on the examine table. I stood there just beyond the door, panting from the hurry and saw what was obviously a very inexperienced "trainee" nervously listening to Chad's heart with a stethoscope. After all we had done to revive him and get him there, this guy was slowly checking his vitals like it was some routine check-up! "Where is the emergency medicine?" I wondered. "Where are the frantic nurses buzzing about? Where is the effort needed to save him?" I stood there momentarily in disbelief—until suddenly I burst through the door and into the room where Chad lay, still unconscious. "You better not let him die!" I shouted. "Do something!"

No sooner had I demanded some action than "she" showed up. I say "she" because the person God sent to help us save Chad was a female. She was wearing fatigue pants and a white tee shirt with dog tags swinging from her neck. She looked like one of those nurses from the TV show M*A*S*H. Immediately she began to take charge, pushing the "trainee" aside and ordering medication. She began to insert a breathing tube down Chad's throat, all the while demanding 50 ccs of this and 20 ccs of that. This woman knew what she was doing and she moved swiftly and with confidence. I felt better right away, until I saw Chad begin to convulse and go into a spasm. "His brain is swelling from the lack of oxygen." I heard her say. "Now everyone out!" She pointed to the door and insisted that I leave.

Reluctantly I complied, turned around, and exited the room. I parted the doors to the sight of my dad. He had changed into dry clothes and arrived at the hospital with my mom. They both shared the same expression of disbelief and shock. How could this have happened? We all felt responsible. I embraced my dad and that is when the emotional gravity of the situation hit me. I broke down and began to cry as he told me that I had done good to help revive Chad. "I was so scared." I sobbed. "It's OK." I heard him say as he patted my back in a gesture that suggested I should pull myself together. I took the cue and made myself stop crying as I walked into a waiting area to be alone. So there I sat, wearing nothing but my swim trunks.

The area was void of any other people and the rest of my family was gathered outside the examining room as the doctor continued to work on Chad. It has been twenty years since all this happened, but I can remember it like it was yesterday. I was sitting in one of the plastic bus station style chairs and I was staring at the floor between my bare feet, holding my head in my hands. I caught the smell of chlorinated vomit and began to cry again. The realization that Chad would spend the rest of his life as a "vegetable" crushed me. He had shown so much promise, such brightness and personality. How could this have happened? "Why Lord?" I asked. That's when I found myself asking God to just let him die. I couldn't bear the thought of seeing him like that. To see him grow up as a bedridden, brain dead "thing" would be too much to stand. It would be a constant reminder of our moment of negligence, a reminder of our "fumble" with God's precious gift. I knew it would devastate my sister, my brother-in-law, my mother, and my father. He would see Chad laying on the bottom of the pool in his dreams, continuously reliving the horror he felt when he first saw him there. My mother would never forgive herself for losing track of Chad, even though it was just for a minute. Everybody would share equally in the blame, the shame, and the guilt of having let this happen. And me, well, I don't think I would ever forgive myself for being uninterested in the search for Chad when he was first realized to be missing. I knew he had suffered brain damage; a small child under water that long would never be the same. I sincerely asked God to take him home.

Suddenly, I heard the distinct sounds of a helicopter coming ever closer to the hospital. The doctor had decided to have Chad airlifted to Columbia, SC, in order to provide better care. There was a large grassy area directly in front of the ER. It was nearly the size of two football fields. In fact, years before it was the very site where I practiced the game as an adolescent. The pain I had endured during those days of tackling practice and endless wind sprints paled in comparison to the site of Chad's little body strapped on that gurney and being hurriedly loaded in the chopper. With a deafening roar and blinding wind, the helicopter pushed off reluctantly toward the sky. It seemed to say, "This is too little, too late." As I turned to shield my eyes, I caught sight of the female doctor who had tried so valiantly to save Chad. She stood there bracing herself against the wind, white tee shirt flapping violently from the blade "wash," dog tags tinkling over her right shoulder. Before the helicopter had even gotten far enough away to hear over the noise, I found myself hugging her neck. I was saying two things by my embrace. One, "Thank you for all you did." Two, "It's OK, you tried your best." She nodded in appreciation for my gesture and fought back tears of her own as she noticed mine. It was as if she knew the pain that lay ahead for us. Remaining silent, she tightened her lips and nodded with a painful acceptance. She felt she could have done more, but he had been under for too long.

Chad's parents jumped in their car to chase down the helicopter as it flew toward Columbia. I must have gone back into shock because I really don't remember riding back home from the hospital. In fact, I don't remember much of anything, except this awful feeling of loss. I suppose I went home to the house full of relatives and tried to comfort them. But, after such clarity and attention to detail for all that had happened before, I really don't remember much of anything until a few hours later when the phone rang.

I dreadfully answered, as I had been expecting my sister's call for the damage report. Once I confirmed it was she, I requested to know right away. I wanted to get it over with. "Well, how bad is it?" I asked bravely. I had every expectation to hear about his brain damage from the extended lack of oxygen, about his vegetative state and grim future. But what I heard next was beyond any and all my imagination could conceive. It was a "Say What?" moment!!

"Mike," my sister said, "Chad is alert and fully conscious." She went on to tell me that when they arrived at Chad's room, he was sitting up in the bed just talking away. There were nurses and doctors gathered around in amazement as he went on in detail about what had happened to him. And the part that still gives me chills to this day is what he said about being in the pool. He woke up saying that he had been at the bottom of the pool with Jesus!! Not only that, but when my dad entered the room, he said he was down there with Jesus when "Papa" came and got him! He went on to tell them about his ride in the helicopter and how Jesus was there too. All I could say in response was "You mean to tell me, he's talking?" "Yes!" my sister replied, "Chad is fine. The doctors say there was no brain damage and he could come home in the morning." I really didn't know what to say. I had been asking God to let him die, thinking it was the only solution. It never crossed my mind to ask for a miracle! What I saw in the natural, Chad's blue lips and lifeless eyes, made me think he was beyond help. He was underwater for at least five to seven minutes. Dad said there were no bubbles coming up at all. The water was flat calm; everything I knew about drowning was evident. Chad was a goner, at least I thought so.

I've read stories about near death episodes and have heard of people having out-of-body experiences during the time when they were clinically dead. Often they speak of a great white light or the presence of Jesus and usually have crystal clear recollections of things that happen around them even though they are "dead." When Chad woke up saying Papa came and got him from the bottom of the pool, I knew he had truly been with Jesus and had seen everything that occurred. Nobody told him this, nobody had the chance to. Nobody told him that he flew in a helicopter, I don't even think he knew what a helicopter was! But Chad was there telling the nurses and doctors all about it. I had to ask God to forgive me for not even thinking He could do this. It never crossed my mind to ask, my faith was small. I say, "was" because I now know that He is able to do exceedingly, abundantly above all we could ever think or imagine and this was such a case.

Chad went on to lead a normal childhood full of sports, school, and every other activity that he was interested in. Today he is a handsome young man, full of faith and willing to tell anyone about the mighty power of God's love.

Twenty years have come and gone since that day at the pool and as I have recalled those events from memory, I'm also reminded of something I used to do. Long before Chad's drowning, I used to take late night swims in that same pool. I would put on a mask to prevent water from going up my nose and I would hang upside down, suspended in the deep end. With my feet just below the surface, I would stretch out and touch the bottom of the pool. My time underwater would grow longer and longer as my breathing would relax and allow me to hold my breath for extended periods of time. The absence of noise would produce an extremely peaceful experience. I would hang there, weightless, in perfect silence, completely still, only coming up for more air, then right back into a position of suspended animation. Sometimes I would do this for more than an hour, it was so relaxing. This was my secret place, my portal to paradise. But I had no idea that it would one day be the place where my Lord and Savior would also decide to spend some time. My spirit soars at the thought of that day, the day when Jesus invited Himself to our pool and saved Chad's life. Thank you Lord, You are mighty in Your mercy and love.

Mike and Chad

THANK YOU JESUS

Well praise you Jesus, the Father's only Son,
You finally brought to pass, the work you had begun.
You touched me in a way that I never felt before.
Touched me deep inside, You came in through the door.
You knocked on my soul, claiming a package sent just
    for me.
You came in Spirit to make a special delivery.
The touch that You gave me will never fade away.
I'm sure I'll not forget what You did for me on the
    special day.

You turned my ashes into beauty, a trade I won't forsake.
You put a smile in my heart, a smile I'll never have to
    fake.
My mourning has turned to
    dancing,
My sorrow flipped to joy.
You've made me feel so fancy,
Like a brand-new baby boy.
So thank you Jesus, you really
    are the most.
**Thank You God in heaven for
    sending Your Holy Ghost!**

ALONE

Alone at last, lastly alone, time has passed, time to go
home
My cellmate has left, picked up by the county.
An outstanding charge, the bondsman was large,
Here to retrieve his bounty.
There were unpaid debts he needed to settle.
More details could have been attained, but I didn't
want to mettle.

My "room dog" was new at this Christianity thing,
An eagle yearning for flight, an eagle with broken wing.
Desire he had to the point of being sad, sometimes he'd
even cry.
I knew his problem, I've played the part, it was a
problem of the heart, promise no lie.
A spirit of criticism was living inside,
Putting down others was his way to hide.
Always finding someone he could put down,
It seemed to be a way of disguising his own heart, which
had a frown.
If it wasn't something about this person or that,
He would often attack me for silly little things,

Like the way I brushed my teeth,
Or even the way I sat!
At first I took it as something wrong with me,
Until later I realized a root of bitterness had grown into
a tree.
The fruit on his branches was easy to see,
It was green with envy and red with jealousy.
No matter how much I shared with him the song
within my heart
He'd often disregard it, casting shadows negative and
dark.

Often I reached out to him, offering my all,
He would say little back or just sit and stare at the wall.
He was here for my deliverance, he witnessed the change.
I did my best to help him make sense of how my spirit
got rearranged.
Assuming this would be good news to my fellow
brother in Christ,
I explained how peace and joy had crushed the former
strife.
This brought him little encouragement as Satan was on
the attack.
Mostly he seemed to ignore me, made me talk to his
back.
Maybe I just talked too much, which I admit was
sometimes the case.

Mostly though he just couldn't relate, the evidence was on his face.

He often mentioned his plans to smoke weed and continue drinking beer,

It was the first thing he wanted to do, once he got away from here.

"But I won't smoke crack," he'd quickly retract, "cause that will bring me back here."

He knew it was true; this was his fourth time through these gates and fences so high.

But those things he still wanted to do will lead to bid number five.

I hope it's not so, I'd hate to see him go this painful route again,

But no matter what you call it, the death penalty is the verdict for sin.

If that's what it takes to get him to cooperate,

The Lord will plow his heart again and again

Until all the rocks of stubbornness have each one been dispelled,

Plucked from the soil in his soul—cast into hell.

Then those roots of bitterness will be pulled one by one.

I've lived through this myself, it "weren't" much fun.

Once it was done, I was no longer on the run.

Allowed to walk for a while.

The wrinkled forehead and gaze of worry replaced with a smile.

This process in me didn't come for free; in fact the cost was quite high.

Not only did I weep and mourn for years on end, but also for it my Jesus did die.

He's the One who made it possible for my life springing brand new.

He did it for me "room dog;" He'll do it for you.

The offer is free; it's plain to see, although not that simple to do.

You've got to die to self, a procedure complicated and cruel.

Allowing some to step on you or being played for a fool.

Contriteness of heart is where it must start and that may take some time.

Saying you're sorry and ceasing to worry is always a positive sign.

I stand in agreement, a suitable case for treatment; you're well on your way.

May God plant you beside living waters, forever you may stay.

I know this will happen, I know it in my heart.

Not for anything I may have given you, although I did my part.

But there is no reason above this fact, God finishes whatever He starts.

So, bye for now "room dog," until we meet again,
I know there were moments of doubt,
But believe me when I say, "You're my friend."

Psalms 91:14-16 (Living Bible)
For the Lord says, "Because he loves me, I will rescue him; I will make him great because he trusts in my name. When he calls on me, I will answer. I will be with him in trouble, and rescue him and honor him. I will satisfy him with a full life and give him my salvation."

IN-BETWEEN JAIL TIME—
JUNE 2005 – APRIL 2008

THE STRANGER

*As you will notice, Mike starts out to tell a story and ends up in a poem mode. That seems to be his most comfortable style of writing.

As it happened to be one day, I was walking down a very long and dusty dirt road. There wasn't a cloud in the sky and the sun shone brightly, as usual, on a mid-summer's day. The heat was interrupted from time to time, only by brief buffetings of wind that would seemingly come from nowhere, causing the moisture on my brow to quickly cool and the dust on the ground to swirl. I kept my focus on the paces before me and spent my attention on the details encrusted in the road. The rhythmic plodding of my feet slowly induced a trance-like state in my mind, as there was little else to do. I had already been walking this road for some time and a quick peek at the horizon told me I still had a ways to go!

But, aside from realizing the distance that lay ahead, I thought I saw the figure of a man also walking this dusty road. He seemed to be opposite me and growing closer with each of our steps. Putting my head

61

back down, I returned to my focus of the ground as it consistently passed beneath. Once again the rhythm encompassed me and I nearly forgot I wasn't alone on this road. I lifted my eyes to check the progress of this man I had seen at such a long way off. But, to my surprise, he had closed the gap considerably and was actually upon me. Hiding just under the bill of my cap, my eyes took quick inventory of this stranger walking along this road with me. His feet were clad with sandals and his attire was simple and plain. He too was very dusty, the road was very dry, and there had been no rain. I glanced at his hands; they were rugged and big, attached to forearms that rippled with veins and notches of muscle. His pace was strong and steady and, although sweaty, he seemed not weary in the least. His hair flowed to his shoulders. His beard was just below the chin. A glance at his face revealed a very confident grin. The moment had come; our paths were about to cross. I prepared to look him in the eyes and acknowledge him with "Hello." But, much to my surprise, he seemed not to notice me at all and actually passed right by without a flinch. With slight dismay, I continued on my way, for the road lay ahead. As quickly as he had appeared he seemed to be gone.

When I heard his voice call me by name, I turned around and nearly fell to the ground, as he was now just behind me. "Don't be afraid," I heard him say, "I have something to show you." His countenance shone like the sun, his eyes sparkled with fire, the smile grew wider and wider. Who was this man and what was he about to show me? How did he guess my name? He doesn't even know me! I thought I could make a stand there in the sand and resist the strangers' gift, but upon parting his garment that covered him, well, my soul began to lift.

As his hands pulled apart, I was amazed in my heart
To see all that was inside him.
There were stars from the sky; I swear I don't lie,
From the brightest to the most dim.
I saw mountains of majesty, valleys that covered thee
With flowers of every kind.
There were eagles in flight soaring,
Lions and tigers in jungles roaring.
I saw creatures from the deep, both great and small,
There was every single kind,
I couldn't count them all.
Volcanoes erupting with red and orange delight,
Blue glaciers melting in every direction,
To the left and to the right.
Sunsets falling, birds calling and each it's own song.
Seasons changing, life rearranging,
Would this last long?

PRISON VISION

I saw laughter replacing tears
And joy being exchanged for fears,
All this done in an instant.
Shame and guilt covered with a quilt
Of mercy and endless love.
Sacrificed on a cross, saving those who were lost,
God's only Son from above.
There were people dressed in white,
Illuminated by His light,
Walking upon golden streets,
Crowns on their heads, no longer stained red:
Throwing them at His feet.
Sounds of great joy and trumpets blasting with sonic
    roar.
I gazed with wide wonder, I wanted to see more.

There were moonbeams and just everything it seemed,
When I felt my knees begin to bend.
I fell down in worship and accepted His friendship
By His hand He did lend.
That's when I noticed the scar from a nail embedded
    in His palm.
There was a wound in His side and tears in His eyes,
As thorns pricked His brow.
With all His power and might He let Himself die,
I just couldn't see how.

THE STRANGER

"I did it for you, believe me, it's true,
So let me complete my task.
I'll be your Lord and Savior no need to beg, just ask."

I felt my soul shiver from the guilty verdict delivered,
Death sentence passed down.
Tears gushed from my eyes, streamed down my face
And puddled on the ground.
I cried, "Jesus, forgive me, excuse my guilt and shame."
With a confident smile, He knew all the while,
With one touch I'd never be the same.

He closed up His chest; He had showed me the best
Of all He ever made.
Gently explaining how His love and mercy
Will never fade.
As all this came to a close,
I struggled to keep myself composed,
But managed somehow, someway.
That's when He winked with a smile,
Said He'd carry me for a while,
And the rest of my days!

John 1:1-5 (NIV)
In the beginning was the Word, and the Word was with
God, and the Word was God. He was with God in the
beginning. Through him all things were made; without

him nothing was made that has been made. In him was life, and that life was the light of men. The light shines in the darkness, but the darkness has not understood it.

SOLD OUT

*I want to add here that what Mike and Rob did on this adventure was exciting and WRONG. They could have suffered severe consequences if they had been caught.

Pearl Jam was coming to Greenville, S.C., and the show was sold out. Initially I had accepted my fate as being "a day late and a dollar short" in regards to my inability to get a ticket. But, as the concert date drew near, I suddenly found myself not only determined to get in, but also inspired to make a special piece of artwork for the band. Without really knowing how I would accomplish this, I quickly began to make a collage from Pearl Jam's VS album and left the rest up to God.

A couple of weeks passed and I had put the finishing touches on the collage when a friend of mine asked me about the concert.

"Ya know Pearl Jam's playing tonight." He said with a mixture of disappointed excitement. Excitement because it was Pearl Jam, disappointment because it was sold out.

"Yeah, I know," I said in return. "And I made them a special collage but have no idea how to get it to them."

Then he suggested we should just go and hang out around the Bi/Lo center, the site for the concert. That's when it hit me, the mother of all ideas.

I said, "No, we're not just going to hang out, we're going there and we're getting in!"

"Yeah, right." He snorted. "That show's been sold out for a month and we're both broke!"

"Well, that may be true, but I've got an idea. How much money do you have?"

"I have 7 bucks," he answered dubiously.

"Perfect!" I exclaimed. Then reaching for a *Circus* music magazine on the way toward the door, I said, "Let's go." Puzzled, yet persuaded from the look in my eye, he followed me out the door without hesitation.

As we climbed into his car with adventurous excitement, I noticed some coax cable on the floorboard. Slamming the door behind me, I picked it up and said, "This will come in handy."

Cranking the car with a smile he said, "What in the world are you getting us into?"

"Trust me," I said, "now take me to Kinko's, I need to make something."

We had no sooner traveled one mile before the radio came blasting through with a concert reminder for the show that night. With a nervous grimace, Rob looked at me, hoping for some sign of reassurance.

"Don't worry, we're gonna get in," I said.

"How?" he fired back.

"Just drive," I ordered.

Arriving at Kinko's, I burst into action. I took the *Circus* magazine, our drivers' licenses and some scissors and tape and headed for a color copier. Within a few minutes I had fashioned together some rather authentic-looking V.I.P. passes. A couple more minutes with the laminator and they were complete.

"Are you crazy?" he quipped.

"Yeah, crazy about Pearl Jam, aren't you?"

"Yeah… but—"

"No buts, just believe."

Reaching the cashier's counter, our total for the copies and supplies was just under seven dollars. So far, so good.

"Now what?" asked Rob.

"Now we head back to my house so we can get dressed and grab the collage I made." Jumping back into the car I began to tell Rob my plan. "Rob, our M.O. is going to be that of two rock-n-roll journalists. We're over here from France on behalf of *Circus* magazine and assigned to report on tonight's concert. I'll take my camera bag and you'll carry this coax cable as if you are my technical assistant."

"Yeah, right, you're gonna get us locked up."

"No, no, I've done this type of thing before. Just follow my lead and if we get in a tough spot remember we're from France and don't speak very good English."

Once we got back to my house, I grabbed a couple of Hendrix Records' tee shirts, my camera bag and the collage I had made for the band. Now, one thing I haven't mentioned yet is that the piece I made for them was not only from their VS album, but also included big bold letters that spelled JESUS, which spiraled around into the center. I used a phrase from some Christian literature for the border that read "It wasn't the nails that held Jesus to the cross, but His love for you and me." I felt an overwhelming urge to use my artwork as a vehicle to witness to the members of the world's most popular band. A daring task? Yes. An impossible one? Maybe. But with God, all things are possible. I had no idea how this would play out, but we were on our way to the biggest concert of the year, at a sold out venue, and masquerading as two journalists from France to boot!!

Just before leaving the house, I went over our M.O. one more time.

"Now, Rob, just carry this coax cable in one hand, this laminated back stage pass around your neck and follow my lead without hesitation. If I make a move to breach security, stick with me as if your job depended on it."

"Job?"

"Yes, your job. I'm a photojournalist and you're my technical assistant. You don't speak English and you are only there to help me. You must convince yourself of this and stay focused. Got it?"

"Got it," he replied with a new look of seriousness. He had imagined his character and was embracing the role.

"If we get caught, just act confused and use broken English to answer any potential questions. And remember we're going to give away some artwork and see the show, not plant a bomb!"

"Oh yeah," he smiled realizing our goal was to have fun, not to hurt anybody.

So, with "costumes" dawned and collage under my arm, we set out toward the Bi/Lo center and the unknown. Rob drove with a silence and a focus that I'd never seen in him before. I said nothing at first… didn't want to distract him. My thoughts raced. Had I made this collage for nothing? Was I insane to think we could infiltrate the inner circle of the most popular band in the world? Were we on our way to jail? Then, with perfect timing, the radio chimed in with another concert reminder. After a medley of Pearl Jam's best songs, the DJ reminded everyone that tonight's show was sold out and even scalpers weren't selling tickets. "So," he said, "If you don't have one, you can hang it up." I glanced at Rob's face long enough to see some doubt rise to the surface. That's when I began to instruct him with my best French accent on the importance of getting in there quickly because we had to get this story submitted in time for the magazine's deadline.

With renewed focus and determination, he nodded and agreed in his best fake French accent. Bursting into laughter, we began to shout and howl out the window as we sped down the road, growing-ever-closer to our destination.

Parking the car a few blocks away, we had arrived early enough, I hoped, to maybe get a chance to deliver the collage firsthand, then sneak our way into the center. The show started at eight and it was only three. We set out on foot with nervous anticipation, not speaking at all. I could sense Rob getting tense, so I calmed him by saying, "Remember, we're not trying to plant a bomb! We're just a couple of Pearl Jam fans who have temporarily gone insane at the thought of missing the show. Desperate times require desperate measures."

"Yeah… and this is freakin' desperate," he said, holding up the coil of coax cable.

Another bout of laughter ensued as we weaved our way through the neighborhood that surrounded the Bi/Lo Center.

Rounding the corner of the last block, the reality of the situation became apparent. There they were, eighteen-wheelers used to transport the stage and all the sound equipment. The tour buses glittered in the sun and flanked the big rigs. A flurry of activity was taking place at the back entrance into the center and security was already in force. Veering off to the right, I led Rob to a vantage point above the loading dock in an attempt to observe the movement of equipment and find a weakness in the security personnel. But, before I could even get us situated, I noticed these two gargantuan men with walkie-talkies pointing directly at us.

"Dang, we've been had already," I sighed to Rob.

"Now what?" he questioned with a voice of disappointment.

"Well, you wait here. I'm going to go down there and just tell them I have something for the band. Maybe they'll give it to them for me. Oh, and here, hold my fake backstage pass for a minute."

I made my way down the hill and then walked through the large gate that enclosed the semi's and tour buses, but since I was carrying the collage, which was nearly 2' x 2', I was quickly headed off by a security guard. Trying to be polite, I attempted to reassure the rent-a-cop that all was well and I just had something for the band.

"They don't want that junk," he said coarsely as he intercepted my progress. Trying to persist, I kept walking toward the tour busses anyway. That's when the two massive and muscular men sprang into action. They began walking toward me waving their arms in a "get-outta-here" type of gesture. Undeterred and partly paralyzed, I stood my ground. That's when I got my first real look into their eyes and realized just whom

I was dealing with. Pearl Jam was worth millions of dollars to a lot of people and these two monsters were there to protect them. Before I knew it, they were upon me and I found myself stuttering and stammering trying to explain that I had some artwork for the band, not a bomb.

"Bomb? What bomb?" one of them scowled.

"No, no. There is no bomb—I, I, I said I've got a piece of art, a, a collage—for the band, see?"

"They don't want that junk," growled the other. "Now—get lost!"

"OK, OK," I pleaded with one hand up and the other clutching my collage.

"OK my rear end." Sneered one of them. "Get lost!"

That's when I abandoned my attempt and went into full retreat mode. I exited the loading zone, tail tucked between my legs, and headed for the safety of my previous position and compadre, Rob.

"What'd they say?" quizzed Rob, as I came near.

"Well, let's just say they weren't interested." I answered.

"Man, they acted like you had a bomb," he said slyly with a devilish grin.

"Yea, tell me about it."

Now I was torn with what to do with the collage; should we still try to sneak in, was I crazy? Maybe we should just go home. Then suddenly I saw the two bodyguards walk toward the entrance of the backstage and disappear into the building. I wondered if they were going to call the police or report me or just what were they doing? We sat motionless for a moment when I noticed this tall, stringy-haired dude coming out from one of the tour buses. He had laminated passes hanging from his neck and I instantly realized he was probably a sound technician for the band.

"Where are you going?" asked Rob as I bolted from our perch and began to make my way back down toward the loading zone.

"Stay put." I shouted as I disappeared down the hill. Without the support from the two goons, I was able to blow right by the rent-a-cop at the gate and approach the sound tech. Looking back on it now, I was definitely flying courageous.

So, by no small miracle, when this sound tech guy saw me, he actually came toward me with a big inviting smile.

"Are you with the band? I asked.

"Yes, I am," he replied with an authentic French accent.

"Do you think you could give this to them?" I asked again while holding up the collage.

"Wow! That's beautiful," he exclaimed. "You made that for the band?"

"Yep, sure did." I replied with nervous disbelief. Before I knew it he rifled it under his arm and headed back toward the tour buses. Soon he was at the door and I nearly fell over as I saw him dissolve into the plush interior contained within the gleaming bus. With a rush of adrenaline and accomplishment, I turned and hurriedly made my way back to Rob. I didn't have to walk very far before he met me coming down the hill with high fives a blazin' and shouts of congratulations.

"Did you see that?" I asked rhetorically.

"Heck ya, dude. You did it. It's in their bus. I can't believe it."

"Me neither. That was awesome!"

The moment was so pure—so predestined—we both became speechless for a second and nearly forgot about the concert, which still lay ahead.

"Now what?" asked Rob with a sense of shocked disbelief.

"I don't know. Let's chill out right here for a minute."

Sitting on the grass, Rob lit a cigarette and then handed back my fake pass with one eye closed to avoid the smoke. I felt so satisfied in that moment, knowing I had been given a vision from God to plant that seed, had the faith to make it, not knowing how or if I'd get it to them, and then to witness it actually happen. I wanted to stay there forever—say nothing—just soak it in. But the concert beckoned and I had to find us a way inside. That's when the second part of this epic adventure began to unfold. I noticed two white vans

76

pull into the parking lot below us and a small army of security personnel began to exit the vehicles. They had on yellow jackets with Security written on their backs and were gathering around this one guy who must have been in charge.

Nudging Rob, I said, "Hey look, that's the ushers and whatnot. They're not with the band, they're local. Our passes might work with them."

Soon their huddle was over and they began to spread out in the direction of the Bi/Lo Center.

"Let's go," I said with determination as I slapped Rob on the arm with the back of my hand. We began to make our way around the building and neared the front entrance, when we both encountered the huge throng of fans that was anxiously awaiting the opening of the doors.

"Ooops! Wrong way. Let's go back around the other way and remember, we're from France and we're on assignment. Got it?"

"Got it," returned Rob.

Then, just as miraculously as the collage hand-off, I noticed a service door halfway between the crowd out front and the "Gorillas" in the back. Reaching for the handle, I gave it a tug and, to my amazement, it popped open! A quick glance at Rob and we made our move. No sooner than we had ducked in the door, I was almost paralyzed by the presence of three people with yellow jackets on and two highway patrol officers. One of the officers instantly threw up his hands and started repeating "Whoa, Whoa, Whoa." Just as quickly as I thought we were done for, I noticed a flight of stairs heading down into the bowels of the arena and began to jog down them saying "It's OK, it's OK," in my best French accent. I figured Rob was going to freeze and chicken out, but to my amazement, he was speaking French too, saying "It's OK, it's OK" while holding up the coil of coax cable. One of the highway patrol began to pursue us down the stairs, but for some reason one of the yellow jackets stepped in front of him and said, "It's OK, they're with the band." Our fake laminated passes had given us just enough of a look that we appeared legitimate. Clopping down the rest of the steps, we pushed open the door at the bottom and never looked back—we were in, but where we were was right in the hustle and bustle of the backstage preparations for that night's show.

A forklift passed by, then a big black box with Pearl Jam stenciled on it nearly ran me over. I continued to walk as if I had to be somewhere important, all the while looking for another door to escape through. With Rob in tow, my eyes darted back and forth simultaneously gazing at all the cool equipment and desperately searching for a place of refuge. Somehow we managed to navigate the chaos of backstage business and began to walk down a corridor. As we entered the large hallway, I noticed a double door to my left and next to the doors, on the right, was an elevator. A quick glance inside the doors left me horrified as my eyes locked dead into the eyes of one of the huge bodyguards I had encountered previously. His eyes widened when he saw me and he started to get up.

"Oh man," I thought, "We're busted! We've got no business back here and the gorillas are on to us!"

Then, to my total shock and relief, the elevator doors sprang open. Without hesitation, as if we had rehearsed it a hundred times before, Rob and I leaped inside. A luxury box waitress pushed her beverage cart in right behind us as I hit the button for the second floor. Time seemed to stand still as I waited for the doors to hopefully close before the goons came to jerk us out. "C'mon baby—close—please, please—whew!" With whisper-like precision the elevator sealed shut and all the hustle and bustle faded away.

Then the waitress noticed our laminated passes and said, "Oh, you two must be in the press box with me!"

Rob's eyes met mine and again, as if prerehearsed, we both nodded and said, "Yes," in our bogus French accents.

"Well then, just follow me," said the skybox waitress, "and I'll show you where it is."

It was all we could do to keep from busting out laughing. How much better could this little adventure get? But little did we know, the best was yet to come!

Our friendly waitress escorted us straight away from the elevator, out and around the concourse, and directly into one of the glassed-in luxury boxes that encircle the Bi/Lo Center. The arena was mostly dark with the exception of a few EXIT signs glowing here and there. We were practically all alone in the vacant concert hall. The waitress told us to make ourselves comfortable while she went to retrieve supplies for the night's work.

Alone at last, safe inside the center, and my collage delivered directly to the band, Rob and I finally let loose with a triumphant laugh of disbelief and relief.

"Ahh!! Can you believe this?" I said with a giggle.

"Man, Mike, you did it … you got us in, this is too much!"

We were so caught up in the moment that neither of realized that while we were slappin' five and laughing like schoolgirls, Pearl Jam had taken the stage to do a sound check.

Suddenly we began to hear the tapping of drums and check one, two's on the mics. A bass thumped and a note was sustained on a guitar. Before long Eddie Veddor himself was on center stage clasping the mic with both hands and humming deep guttural moans. Chills ran up and down my arms as I sank down in my chair to avoid detection and prepared myself to witness the unimaginable: a chance to eavesdrop on the hottest band in the world doing a sound check with nobody in the Bi/Lo Center except me and Rob. We both glanced at each other quickly in disbelief, gritting our teeth and grinning with the same shared thought—"Is this really happening?!" But before we could say a word, Pearl Jam ripped into "Even Flow" and a deafening roar echoed throughout the arena. I leaned over and shouted Heavy Metal Thunder in Rob's ear. We slapped five and clasped hands raised in victory as our bodies bobbed to the pulsating rhythm. We could finally shout and laugh just like we did in the car on the way here, but this time Pearl Jam wasn't on the radio, they were right in front of us!! A medley of other songs followed, then, just as quickly as they had appeared they were gone, leaving us spellbound, mouths agape and ears ringing.

What could possibly happen next? I wasn't even able to finish asking myself that question when I heard the voice of our friendly skybox waitress. At first I thought she had figured us out and was going to ask us to leave. But instead she said, "Hey guys, I've got my supplies, can I fix you two something to drink?"

"Sure." I replied. "I'd like a ginger ale."

Rob perked up and requested a screwdriver!

"Comin' right up," she smiled.

A few seconds later we were handed our beverages and encouraged to make ourselves comfortable. So there we sat, like two Cheshire cats, grinning from ear to ear and feeling on top of the world. That's when I began to think that this was all too good to be true and maybe we shouldn't press our luck.

"Hey Rob, let's make like a tree and split."

"Yeah," he agreed. "Let's not push our luck."

And with that, we thanked our friendly hostess, apologized for not being able to tip her because we were flat broke, and made a clean getaway. And the timing couldn't have been better because just as we exited the luxury box the doors opened and a flood of rambunctious fans poured in. Still fearing the two gorillas, we made use of the mob and blended in.

Weaving in and out among the crowd, I felt like the king of the world. I could see the anxious excitement on the many faces that whizzed past me like so many cars on a busy expressway, each one oddly unique, yet all sharing an expression of anticipation for the soon-to-start show. People seemed to glow, a sense of gratitude that the "music gods" had granted them access to be a part of this event. I noticed a sea of faces peering in from beyond the windows that separated the outside from us. They looked on with desperate agony—they had failed to make it in and they knew they were going to miss the show. That's when I got the biggest sense of superiority, a sense of elation, a sense of "if you all only knew." For the ones who were in with me and eager to hear Pearl Jam live, well I had already heard them—Rob and I had been two flies on the wall—privy to something millions of people would "kill" for. And for me, I had successfully gotten my custom-made artwork on the tour bus. I was on cloud nine. All I had left to do was enjoy the show. From this point on, it was all gravy. More like gravy on top of gravy.

Of all the concerts I had been to, from KISS in 1978, Aerosmith countless times, Heart in the '80s, Metallica in the early '90s, and Smashing Pumpkins a handful of times—The Black Crowes—Ted Nugent—Lynard Skynard—Styx—Foreigner—Foghat—and even Grand Funk, the crowd at this particular show was unique. There was a sense of shared camaraderie. An electricity that was so tangible. I could practically taste it. It was as if we all knew each other or had been through similar experiences or something. A general sense of unity, a brother/sisterhood. A scattered family reunited by one common cause, the music of Pearl Jam! We were there to celebrate. Celebrate being there. Celebrate being alive, some by pure luck, some by fate, some by the grace of God. But all the same, alive. I was there as a stowaway of sorts and we were all about to set sail on an unknown, highly anticipated voyage with Eddie Vedder as the captain. We would be the colors available for his artistic impression, ready to be painted in a glorious kaleidoscope of human faces and expressions, willing and eager to lend our lives temporarily for his use. People were laughing and hugging each other everywhere I looked. The place was packed to capacity, hardly an inch to move; yet nobody seemed bothered in the least at our sardine-like state.

At one point, before the show got started, Rob and I had wiggled our way onto the floor and were standing shoulder to shoulder with a couple thousand other smiling faces, when a chain reaction occurred.

Somehow a mass of people in front of us fell backwards and, like dominoes, a wave of falling bodies swept towards us. Unable to move in either direction, there was nothing we could do except fall also. People fell on me, then I fell on people around me. Before I knew it, three or four hundred of us were laying in a tangled mass of humanity. I expected to see angry faces everywhere as some people spilled their beverages and others, complete strangers, lay on top of each other. But, as I said before, this was a unique crowd and nobody seemed to mind at all. In fact, we all just laughed and began helping each other up, as did those around us who didn't fall. I never thought an audience of that size could be so singularly minded. No sooner had we gotten to our feet than the lights went out and the stage began to glow with the red lights of amplifiers accented with a bluish-green hue from colored overhead lighting!

The crowd roared and chills ran up and down my entire body. This was it!! Pearl Jam was ready for lift off and I was at ground zero… smack dab in the middle of the floor and about twenty rows away from the stage. Rob and I took one last look into each other's eyes, sharing a mutual expression which read loud and clear, "We did it, now let's ROCK!" Without hesitation the ripping intro for "Even Flow" came screaming across the arena. The driving bass and thunderous drums came in right on time and the entire audience leapt into the air in unison and began to mash. High fives and air guitars simulations were everywhere as people closed their eyes in ecstatic jubilation and cast off every care, getting completely lost in the moment. This was the last thing I noticed as I too closed my eyes and joined in the friendly melee. The sound was like thunder, crisp, clean and note for note. It really was Pearl Jam, we had made it in and they were just getting started.

No sooner had the first song ended, with the crowd roaring with approval, than they tore into "Animal" for their second offering. Instantly recognizing this song from the VS album, Rob turned to me and said, "Pick me up." A strange request it may seem, but I knew what he wanted to do. With a crowd that thick, that frenzied, crowd "surfing" was a no-brainier and Rob wanted to be the first. Before he could even finish telling me to, I bent down, wrapped both arms tightly around his knees and hoisted him up over my shoulder. I thought he'd be tossed around for a bit then land safely next to me once the crowd had finished with him. Boy was I wrong! No sooner had I gotten him above my head than he was thrust forward toward the stage as if on a high-speed conveyor belt. A look of mixed terror and delight lit up his face as I watched him evaporate into the crowd.

"Rob!" I yelled, as if I could retrieve him with a shout. But it was too late, the crowd had their first sacrificial lamb and worked together with coordinated precision, flinging him over the barricade and sending him cartwheeling onto the stage. Slightly dazed and disoriented, Rob lay motionless on his back just long enough for Eddie Vedder to chime in with the next lyrics from "Animal," which were "why would you want to hurt me?" as he bent over Rob with the mic stand in hand. Rob threw up both hands with fingers spread as if to say, "I don't want to hurt you." Then he scrambled to his feet and literally dove off the stage, back over the barricade and into the crowd, who cheered with delight and satisfaction. Separated by the pulsating crowd, finding Rob became an impossibility. I figured I'd see him at the car after the show. My concern for just how or if I'd find him soon dissipated as I lost myself back into the music and live performance of the band.

So there I was, neck deep in smashing Pearl Jam fans, sweaty already, and all alone. But, as I said before, this crowd was united, so it was easy to connect with those around me and continue my celebration. A few more songs and the undulating movement of the mob, I started to become dizzy from the heat being generated as well as from exhaustion.

It became very apparent to me that I needed to get some fresh air and get it soon. I literally had to "swim" my way off the floor and climb the stairs leading to the concourse before I felt the relief of fresh conditioned air. The cool air, combined with the dampness of my clothes, hit me like a five gallon bucket of water being thrown directly in my face.

A quick trip to the concession stands for an ice-cold soda and I was revived. The music from inside the arena beckoned, but I wasn't quite ready for the relentless action taking place on the floor. I decided to circle around and catch a view from behind the stage. I walked briskly, finishing off the last available liquid from my soda. Once only the ice remained, I skipped into a run, slinging the cup and cubes on the floor without any regard for the trash can as I blurred right past. This miniature time-out from the action inside was necessary, but I felt over-joyed at the chance to bask once again in all that was and is a Pearl Jam performance. Parting the double doors that opened into section "XYZ," the warmth from the crowd and some thunder from the band hit me like a linebacker.

I jogged down the steps and squeezed into the seats behind stage to check out the action. It wasn't long before the frenzied activity on the floor in front of me began to beg for my attendance. I resisted as long as I could, remembering the heat from the mashing and the cramped conditions. Then I took a gazeful gander into the crowd in front of the stage. What I saw will stand out in my mind forever. A memory burnt into my brain like a psychotic pirate C.D. It was an undulating sea of smiling faces, contorted with intensity from each new riff and note played by the band. There were outstretched hands reaching desperately toward the stage as if they begged for the last life jacket on the Titanic. The inexpressible joy that was felt by all had manifested itself into these air-grasping attempts to touch the band members. It literally looked like a two thousand-seat roller coaster had rested the largest hill on the ride and was plunging downward at 100mph fast approaching a double-corkscrewed loop! I've never seen anything like it nor do I expect to ever see it again. One hundred percent participation by everyone within earshot of Pearl Jam's crunchy flavored, riff laden, vocal shredding style of music. All I could say to myself was, Wow! My new position behind stage could no longer hold me; I had to rejoin the fray. Somewhere within the churning melee was Rob. Was he all right? Was he looking for me? Was he alive? Never mind, I had to get back in there and I had to do it then.

Before I could even process all I was witnessing, I felt my legs straighten, propelling me out of my seat and back around the concourse. I soon found the same spot I used for my earlier escape and parted the doors. Again the sound hit me like a wave and the heat from the floor sucked me in like a moth to a candle. I used my fake pass to push past the ushers and gained access to the raucous crowd. I was in the back at first, where the action was not as intense, but I found it unsatisfactory.

I needed to get myself back into the thick of it, so I took a deep breath and ducked my head, plowing straight forward into the mass of humanity. It was literally like swimming in a pool of people all jumping and grooving to the music. I popped my head up for a second to check my progress. I was still only about halfway in, not close enough, I thought. Another deep breath and I made my second assault. No more than two or three steps into this attempt and I ran headlong into someone plowing through the crowd in the opposite direction. I literally had to put my hands up to keep from bumping head to head and he did the same. Simultaneously we looked up as if into a mirror. And I'm here to tell you, hand raised to God, it was Rob!

"Mike!" he yelled with astonishment.

"Rob!" I echoed back.

He was shirtless, glistening with sweat and beet red in the face! To my surprise, especially since his shirt was gone, he had managed to preserve his laminated pass. He was on his way out for the same reason I had abandoned the floor earlier… survival. After bumping into me like he did, he did an about-face and led our charge back into the middle by yelling over his shoulder, "Follow me."

I grabbed him by the back of his belt and we forced our way toward the front. Our movement maxed out about 20 feet from the barricade, almost exactly where we had first been separated. Content with our location, we stopped trying to get any closer and returned to our celebration. We were lost but now we were found and we were in the middle of a Pearl Jam concert at a sold out Bi/Lo Center!

The play list rolled on; the band was as relentless as they were flawless. Vedder howled, McCready squealed, and Ament's bass would nearly suck the air from your lungs between each thump. Before I knew it, I was soaking wet and limp as a dishrag from all the dancing, mashing, and catching of each new crowd surfer. Three encores later and the show was over. The crowd, myself included, was stuck somewhere between wanting more and welcomed relief. Pearl Jam had held us in their grip and we had been at their mercy. They could have played 'til the next day and nobody would have even considered leaving. The show was epic! Nobody headed for the exits at first. People stood around and exchanged high fives and group hugs all around me. There was a sense of having been baptized into a new life, a life post-Pearl Jam.

With our ears ringing and jeans wet with sweat, Rob and I stood there breathless watching the crowd slowly thin out and reluctantly make their way off the floor and toward the exits.

"Dude, where's your shirt?" I quizzed.

"Man, it got ripped off me around the third song. Everybody kept grabbing for my passes, but I managed to hang on to them somehow," explained Rob.

"Let's see if we can find it," I said as I noticed other people picking up clothes from the other side of the barricade.

I'll never forget the sight once we reached the barrier and looked over its edge. Clothes, lots of clothes. There was a pile of clothes nearly waist deep and running the entire width of the stage! All of them were wet and could only lay there in a heap, helpless and abandoned. Each article had a story to tell and I knew what it was. They were the remnants; the remains from a two thousand-seat roller coaster ride piloted by Eddie Vedder and Co. A hurricane had blown through Greenville, S.C., and its name was Pearl. The clothes were crammed against the stage, all in a Jam. This was the telltale signature—it was Pearl Jam. They had rocked the crowd right out of their clothes and shoes and hats, literally!! Rob looked at it with the same conclusion.

"We'll never find that shirt."

So he selected a new garment, a long-sleeved, paisley-covered satin shirt; it was an upgrade for his trade. I grabbed a canvas fishing cap, it fit perfectly on my head. With a mutual grin of total satisfaction, we spoke together… "Let's go home!"

The walk back to the car was effortless. We were on cloud nine and nothing would be finer. Once inside the car, Rob and I remained silent—there was nothing to say. Words couldn't be found to describe what we had just experienced. It all happened so fast, so furiously.

With a willing hum, the car's engine came to life and the radio was still on from our arrival. With perfect timing, the DJ made mention of the concert. He announced that the show had been stellar, that Pearl Jam had exceeded the hype. Then he apologized to all the fans who were unable to get tickets and missed the show. With a pop-eye grin, Rob glanced at me. I returned the look with a wink and a smile of my own. We had done it! Mashing the accelerator, Rob drove us into the night, officially ending our dream date with Pearl Jam. It had been a night to remember and it was one I'll never forget.

Sample of Mike's collages

New Year's Eve

Maybe it was '02 or maybe it was '03;
Exact dates aren't for sure, but it was definitely New
     Year's Eve.
The end of one year and the beginning of the next
Is not the focus of this poetic text.
For it was on this night that I got such a horrific fright,
It was one of those nights that nearly cost me my life!
The years preceding had been ones of struggle and pain
The life I was leading was controlled by addiction to
     cocaine.

The setting for this true rendition
Was a house in the South in tattered condition.
Residue Ronnie was its master
And the dealers who came and went had the drugs I
     was after.
Despite many attempts to stay away,
I'd always seem to wind up there regardless of how hard
     I'd pray.
I had this particular habit of dropping by late at night,
     sometimes after work.

PRISON VISION

Usually it would involve leaving my wife home alone
    like a total jerk.
I'd dip in and dip out, driving away with the dope I'd
    bought hidden in my mouth.

The disappointment of relapsing was my primary
    thought.
Second on the list was the fear of getting caught.
But those concerns became wishful thinking,
As this night of remembrance still leaves me with a
    feeling in my stomach sinking.
I had worked 'til well past one, I stayed until every
    delivery was done.
This should have been my cue to head for home to
    snuggle with my wife waiting for me all alone.
But it was New Year's Eve and time was fading fast
I decided to celebrate, stop by Ronnie's and get one
    quick blast.

I hoped and I wondered if he'd be at home.
As I entered the house, I found him there but he wasn't
    alone.
Sitting on the couch, this guy was there.
I didn't recognize his face, as I tried not to stare.
But I did notice the scars that adorned his evil glare.
Ronnie stood motionless as if frozen in fright.
The look on his face, like a deer caught in headlights.
I didn't take his countenance as a sign

New Year's Eve

Cause I only had one thing on my mind.
Was this guy on the couch a dealer or just another
    slouch?
I'd find out with one question asked.
Get what I wanted and accomplish my task.
"What's up?" I quizzed. "Are you straight?"
But instead of the usual nod, his eyes focused on me,
    full of hate.

Instantly I felt something was amiss.
He stood up, larger than life and with clenched fists.
That's when I realized I had invited the Devil to dance.
All around the room my eyes began to glance.
But before I could move or attempt to run
This tango with Satan had already begun.
He snatched me up and pushed me against the wall.
The dude was easily six-four and reeked like alcohol.
His eyes were cold and black, his face scarred from
    previous attacks
A look of disgust and total disdain
Seemed to be the result from his years of pain.

"Give me your money, you mother ------."
This was his command as my body began to pucker.
Rifling through my pockets, I began to resist.
Then I noticed the knife held in one of those clenched
    fists.

PRISON VISION

I'm sure I turned the palest white as I prepared to lose
my life.
He seemed to enjoy the fact that I had fallen so easily
into his trap.
My lip trembled with fear and loathing,
Would they find me behind the house rotting and
bloating?
"Yes, just take it," I pleaded, not trying to be funny.
With dollars in one hand and a knife in the other,
He covered my mouth violently and attempted to
smother
Any sound I could make or shouts for help
His hand was dirty and with it over my mouth it was
easily smelt.

This entire moment had come so suddenly,
I was only able to escape because God was watching
over me.
But before he ever considered turning me lose,
I had to stand there for what seemed like an eternity
And smell his breath of 100 proof.
My stomach dropped and my heart stood still;
I was at his mercy being held against my will.
He had my money but seemed like he wasn't sure what
else to do.
Should he strangle me or take his knife and run me
through?

Seconds felt like hours as he stood over me imposing
  like a tower.
Unbridled fear and shock had me paralyzed;
This was a common situation found in a dope house,
  but never realized.

Then, just when I was sure he'd lacerate my liver,
I felt myself get faint and knees begin to quiver.
He sneered his lip and laughed with an evil gesture;
Deciding to leave and find someone else to pester.
As he walked out the door with a drunken stagger,
I bent over with relief and forgot about what I was after.
Then I noticed Ronnie conveniently tucked out of sight,
Apparently this guy had been there and doing this all
  night.
"Gosh, Ronnie," I quipped. "You could have said
  something, anything would do"
Then he said, "Are you crazy? I ain't no fool.
That man is mean as a snake and over six feet tall.
He woulda hurt me bad if I said anything at all."
That's when I realized no high was worth my life, which
  was just given back
Definitely worth more than $40 or a few pieces of crack.

I tucked my tail and drove out of the hood –
Swore I'd never return, I was done for good.
But cocaine is a drug without remorse,
Once you're on it, you'll return to the source.

PRISON VISION

Regardless of how ugly it gets or dangerous the spot,
The person you used to be will all but be forgot.
You'll risk your life and walk train tracks in the rain,
You'll keep coming back despite the cost, the destruc-
  tion and the pain.
Playing high stakes poker with no aces up your sleeve
Like the gamble I took on this particular New Year's
  Eve.

I could have been stabbed and left for dead.
Other times I was robbed with loaded guns to my head.
But each time I walked away without a scratch,
For compared to God the Devil is no match.
Grace and mercy have sustained my existence,
Jesus looked after me with vigilant persistence.
And know that I'm able to realize the danger I've been
  carried through
I decided to share this story with anyone interested—
  Are you??

GEORGIA,
FLOYD COUNTY JAIL–
MAY 2008 – SEPTEMBER 2008

KILLIN'

This killin' time is killin' me,
I'm so blind, I can hardly see.
What I've done appears to be
A dirty down and low one.
No one wants to trade with me,
Now I find time's doin' me.

Well I should cry myself to sleep but I'll try;
I'll try to be with Thee.
So Lord I'm needin' someone,
Guide my mind under an old shade tree
Won't you guide my mind—tranquility?
Go ahead and come on,
Take this heavy load from me.

It's sublime; it's cruel and mean
Sittin' round locked up in Floyd County.
I'm like a rhyme, like a mystery.
Locked behind this door, in cellblock "G"

KNOW JESUS

You tell me that you want to know Jesus,
Is that what you're trying to say?
Looking down from heaven He sees us
And helps us out along the way.

I've got to say—say
That there is no other way,
He hears me pray—pray
Gives me what I need each day.

Now if you're saying "no" to Jesus,
There's some trouble on the way.
A place of weeping that never ceases,
A place where there is hell to pay.

Can you be saved—saved?
It doesn't have to be this way.
He made a way—way
He wants to save your soul today.

KNOW JESUS

When you come to know Jesus,
He'll touch you in a special way,
He'll give you plenty of reason
To sing His praises every day.

He is the way—way
Listens to me when I pray.
Don't run away—way
Listen to me when I say.

FLIES

Sitting here with thoughts that bleed, surrounded by
    negativity,
Can't accept this as my reality.
If I could only break these bars and fly,
I wouldn't have to compromise.
Instead I'm sitting here like wet ashes with X's in my
    eyes,
I'm drawing flies.

These things I see, can't accept or believe,
Satan's always coming at me with his lies.
Push away from TV trying its best to bewilder me.
I won't accept this fate no matter how hard he tries.
Will it make the blind to see
A view from mountain tops of Tennessee?
Can it gush some water from a well that's dry?
Trying hard to conform and comply.
Sitting here like wet ashes with X's in my eyes,
I'm drawing flies.

FLIES

Jesus come and rescue me,
I'm calling on the Trinity.
Rain down your power from the skies
Take away these wet ashes and X's in my eyes.
Chase away the flies.

PRAYER;

Dear Jesus,

Hear my prayer, oh Lord—for in You I trust. You've shown me new things each day and kept me safe the whole way. Help me accept whatever happens to me concerning the possibility of being transferred Monday or Tuesday. The chances are high but I don't want to be disappointed, Lord. I've been as patient as I could and willing to learn from You during this time here. Thank you for all You've done so far for me in this very trying situation. I've seen Your hand at work and praise You for letting me see it. Prepare my heart for all that lies ahead; both in here and on the day You set me free again. Help my cellmate, Mr. Kelly, keep his focus on You and Your love. Thank you for allowing me this time with him. Help me to help him once I get out. I praise You for who You are, how You are, what You did, and all that You're going to do. You are my Savior, my King, and my Lord. I am sincerely grateful for all You've done for me. Amen

MESSAGE

I've gotta get a message to Jesus.
I've got somethin' I need to say.
It can't get there on no bus ride,
Can't get there on no plane.
I don't want to wait for tomorrow,
I've got to get it through today.

I need to pray—pray
Fall down on my knees and pray
I'm gonna pray—pray
Tell Him what I've got to say.

Life is full of temptations,
Coming at you every day.
If you're not very careful,
You'll get stuck in miry clay.

Just know there's a solution,
Listen to what I say.
Cry out now to Jesus,
Ask Him for your debt to pay.
He'll be there like a friend,

PRISON VISION

Help you out along the way.
Don't put it off for tomorrow,
Don't find no games to play.
Get down on your knees right now,
Open up your mouth and say.

CHILDREN

Our Father who art in heaven, allow me to know Your
  name,
Let Your will be made clear, shine Your light, remove
  my shame.
Give me Your way each and every day,
This is what I want to preach and say.
I can't wait to see Your face,
To feel Your love, to feel Your embrace.
For the times I've known it,
But didn't talk too much about it.
Forgive me Lord, for living like a refugee.
For allowing myself to be set adrift,
Floating aimlessly in an endless sea.
Any part in the storm was my excuse to set sail,
Living outside the norm, knocking on the gates of hell.
You've placed me back on solid ground,
I can see Your grace each time I look around.
Let me not be tempted to fall,
I give these cares to You, You can have them all.
Thank you, Jesus, for what You've done,
I submit this prayer to You, Father, Holy Ghost, and
  precious Son.

BAINBRIDGE, GEORGIA,
DRUG REHAB PROGRAM–
OCTOBER 2008 –
MARCH 2009

OUT SHINED

I just looked out the window, things aren't lookin' so
   good,
Well, I'm lookin' California, but I'm feelin' Minnesota.
I'm lookin' in the mirror and the reflection's getting
   colder.
I'm thinkin' much younger, but I'm slowly getting older.
So now you know who gets mystified.
So now you know who gets teary-eyed.
Show me the power Lord, 'cause I'd like to know,
See I'm down on my knees today.
It gives me the butterflies; hear me, I pray,
'Cause I'm down on my knees today.
I'm feeling out shined, out shined, out shined.

Well, I just looked in a window, and things are feeling
   so good,
I'm movin' right along now, doing everything that I
   should.
I'm looking at the floor now, but my thoughts are on
   the ceiling.
And I'm writing all these words down, so I can tell You
   how I'm feeling.

PRISON VISION

Show me the power cord; I'd like to play, 'cause I'm
down on my knees again,
It gives me the butterflies—gives me a way—and it
keeps me alive today.
I'm feelin', ohh I'm feelin' out shined, out shined, out
shined.

COLOR BLIND

I had the most interesting conversation the other day. It started out simple enough with the usual things people say to fill empty spaces that often occur. You know, stuff like "Boy, it's nice outside," "Yeah, sure is," bla, bla, bla. Then my friend noticed a swarm of gnats about twenty feet away. He became fascinated by the way they would lift off from the grass, form into an undulating glob, then spiral down like a funnel back into the grass. Soon I became mesmerized by their repeated motion of rest, lift off, swirling flight, and funneling return. Our conversation soon faded as their movement and ballet-like dance slowly hypnotized us both.

Then my friend Nick says, "Just think if aliens came to our planet and observed us in the same way. If they hovered above a major city, we might appear to them just like those gnats appear to us."

"What if we tried to talk to the aliens, but instead of hearing all of our different syllables and voice inflections, they just heard blips and burps like some form of high-tech Morse code?" I said.

Then he said, "What if they didn't hear any distinct sounds at all? What if they could only hear our intentions?!"

"Dude!" I said, "What an awesome concept! What if our intentions were seen as colors flowing from our mouths? Red would be for anger or hateful intentions, blue for genuine and honest things, green for peaceful and gentle words, yellow for pain and sadness, orange for joy and happiness. Laughter would look like rainbow-colored music notes and miscellaneous cymbals. Black would pour out like tar if we spoke evil and blasphemous things."

We both laughed and enjoyed the complete randomness of our conversation, then shrugged it off as we returned to work.

But now, after about a week of reflection, I've come to realize something very profound. You know, Jesus was always emphasizing that what matters most to God was the inner part of a man, or what is in a man's heart. He warned the Pharisees by saying their outward appearance and lofty words seemed to be clean and holy, but through His ability to see into their hearts, He was convinced that their mouths were like "open graves." The contradictions that occurred when they "spoke" of heavenly things, yet harbored hatred, malice, deceit, pride, envy, and other blasphemies in their inner man smelled like rotting flesh. After my conversation with Nick, I've come to see Jesus as the great supernatural being, similar to the fictional aliens we spoke of who couldn't have cared less about our syntax, but only hears the intentions of our heart—my heart.

Lord, I thank you for this illustration of how You work. I pray that I won't fool myself with clever syntax. I also thank You for paying my debt by way of the cross. It was an insurmountable "sin tax." Amen

COURAGEOUS

I've just got to find a way to tell the world about You,
Of all Your love for us, no one could ever doubt You.
Of all Your graciousness and tender mercy,
The way You died for us on hills of Calvary.

So you could fly me—courageous
You've stood beside me—courageous

You know I've seen the things that people seldom live
    through.
They tried to smash my dreams and pull me away from
    You.
But now I'm standing here to claim Your witness.
You never left my side, You showed me kindness.

So fly me—courageous
You sacrificed Thee—courageous

COURAGEOUS

Now that it's come to pass, assignment written.
I stood my ground, firm and fast, twice shy, once bitten.
This was the way for me to know Your mercy.
I owe it all to Thee, You never tried to hurt me.

So fly me—courageous
Stand beside me—courageous
I pledge my life to Thee—courageous
You sacrificed Your life—courageous

SAY WHAT?

It caught me off guard once I realized just what you
    had said—
Something about being able to comprehend and
    explain all the Scripture I'd read.
You wished you could understand them just like me,
So I've decided to write this poem so maybe you'll see
That what I've come to trust and know to be true
Was not fun to be done or easily lived through.

The paths that were taken while going my own way
Is what the Bible describes as a sheep gone astray.
It wasn't my intention to come under attack.
I was overconfident and thought I'd find my own way
    back.
But once I was lost and it became impossible to see,
I found myself crying, "Lord Jesus, please come and
    save me."
For the waves had crested and the boat was adrift.
The student was tested; I'm here to admit.
I wanted to end my voyage through hell,
The story was sad and I knew it all too well.

SAY WHAT?

My best friend's life had ended by suicide,
I considered it myself, but couldn't decide.
Thinking I had made sense of it all,
I failed to realize that the mountain was too tall.
Trying to ignore and bury the pain,
I did not realize the game had changed.

Addiction soon followed and was there to stay,
Feeling empty and hollowed from day to day.
"Lord, I just want to sit here next to Your cross,
Please help me forget this grief and this loss.
For he was my friend and I miss him dearly.
Help me understand or see this more clearly."
I'm still wondering what he was thinking and why?
But he's gone forever with no chance for good-bye.

But now, what I've come to believe and accept in my
    heart—
His suicide was ground zero where my education would
    start.
To become familiar with suffering and pain,
A way to find answers for questions so hard to explain.
Without my introduction to real life tragedy,
I may have never unraveled the Scripture's mystery.
Or to know what it's like to be lost and refound,
Or scream out all night without making a sound.

PRISON VISION

This is just one of my lessons offshore.
I've got dozens to share, want to hear more?
Which one should I choose? The choices are there.
Novels of sorrow, chapters filled with despair.
I always thought it would eventually end, surely it
    couldn't last.
But since his death, nearly twenty years have passed.
I've wrestled with demons, gone nights without rest,
Walked with reckless abandon through the valley of
    death.

I've shared tears with the wounded, touched hearts that
    were broken.
I've seen cancer removed from prayers that were spoken.
I've been carried across the abyss of the night,
Forgetting any thought about ending my life.
I've lost things I loved and forgotten names that I
    knew.
Felt God's Holy Spirit descend like a dove, then evapo-
    rate like the dew.
But one thing I did that never ended or ceased
Was trusting in Jesus to bring me sweet relief.

So to ask me now, if miracles are real
Is beyond all I can imagine or begin to feel.
And to say, "One day you'd want to be like me!"
Makes me tremble with fear and get weak in the knees.
For Satan has tried his best to deny

SAY WHAT?

The love that I feel when I look to the sky.
I can't walk on water or turn it to wine,
But what I can do is tell you about this life of mine.

I once was a sinner, self destructive and bound for hell.
But He never gave up on me; regardless of the times
    I fell.
And now that I'm here at the place of reflecting,
I'm convinced beyond a shadow's doubt,
That it was God who's done the protecting.
I had tried my best to waste this life of mine,
But at the end of every wrong turn,
It was always Him that I'd find.
I thought it not fair to be given this plan,
Or to finish this race from where it began.
But looking back on it all,
It's what I needed to become a man.

Now I'm feeling such joy inside me,
The Devil's done dealing, I'm finally free
To love once again with a heart that was shattered and
    broken,
To make new friends and help blind eyes reopen.

To point to the One who carried me here,
The One who gave me courage in place of my fear.
So if you still want to be just like me,
You'll have to have been held captive before you can
    go free.

PRISON VISION

I hope and I pray these roads you won't walk,
But they are the reason I speak of Jesus when I talk.

For every toil, snag, and snare,
I'm one hundred percent convinced that Jesus was
    there.
To lift up my head and keep me going
Up and over that mountain without ever knowing
Why it was so, or had to be.
But He used it all as a chance to demonstrate
His endless love for me.

All my train-wreck disasters that went up in ash
Have been replaced with laughter,
My mourning turned to dance.
I found Him beautiful, what more could I ask?
I'm so excited about my future that I couldn't care less
    about my past.
I can't show you the trauma or scars on my heart,
But I could write a book and this is how it will start.
If I tried to tell you everything He's done for me,
It'd be like counting drops of water in an endless sea.
I could go on and on with this story and plot,
I could write a poem entitled "Say What?"
But instead I'll end it with a favorite Scripture, just
    one...
"For God so loved the world that He gave His only
    begotten Son."

ALLEN'S STORY

Allen and Mike had been best friends since high school. When they were seniors, Allen's parents moved to Texas, but Allen wanted to graduate from the school that he had been attending for so long. We invited him to come live with us, which really bonded them. All this time they were smoking marijuana unbeknownst to my husband and me. After graduation (which Allen's parents attended) Allen said good-bye, keep in touch, etc., and drove off with his parents. He joined the Army for 2 years while Mike attended college in Sumter, played baseball, and hung out with other guys who were around.

By the time that Allen had completed his Army time, Mike was attending the University of South Carolina. Allen wanted to be a surgeon and wanted to attend school with Mike, so he came to South Carolina and they got an apartment together. They would come "home" every couple of weeks (we lived about 30 miles away) to wash clothes, eat some home-cookin', hang out with friends, and do drugs. By this time I was aware of what was going on!!

It was a weekend in March 1991 that Allen decided to take his fateful ride across the US. Mike had gone to Daytona to see the Motocross race and was not aware that Allen was gone. I got a call from the police in California looking for Allen's parents. At the second call, I asked them to please tell me what they needed, and they told me that he had committed suicide!! Later that evening Mike called me to tell me how good the race was and how excited he was. I knew if I didn't tell him then that he would never forgive me, so I told him. He started hollering and crying, just like I knew he would.

The part that was so unreal was that Allen had a tape recorder beside him all the way to California and he talked to Mike all the way!! He mailed it before he did the "deed" and Mike received it several days after we learned of his death. He also took pictures. He told Mike that he was lonely, depressed, didn't have any money, never heard from his family, and wanted to see what death was like!! He also told Mike what to do with his things. Mike kept his bed.

Another thing that made it so unreal was that his parents had him cremated in California, and his ashes sent to Texas for burial, so we had no closure. We had a memorial service at our church where Allen was a member, but it was so unreal. Mike never got over Allen's death and he tried to bury his pain with opiates. They were both 24 years old.

THE DAY YOU DIED

I want to write a poem to all the people that don't even
know him.

He was my best friend, name was Al.

We went to school together, he was my number one pal.

He was full of life—he was animated.

But slowly he became convinced that it was all overrated.

It seemed useless, he was searching for answers, but he
was clueless.

So he got up the nerve to do this—a thing called suicide.

He got in his car and took a ride all the way to the
other side

Of the country—west coast—California.

I'm writing this down to inform ya.

It was a bad decision, a horrible idea—miscalculated
conclusion.

It still hurts my brain like a bruise,
deep-rooted contusion.

News of his death brought
confusion.

Allen Chambers

127

PRISON VISION

I was saddened, angry with myself, and maddened.
I wanted to fight, beat the world, and say, "It ain't right."
I was devastated, turned the pain inward, told myself
    I was hated.
"You should have known, you calloused coward."
I projected guilt on myself, malice in fast forward.
I became self-destructive and pitiful,
Like an over-used latrine, I was miserable.

Acted reckless—couldn't care less—was in total distress.
Stuck for days on my mattress.
I didn't want to get up, wanted to give up,
But life goes on, every morning a new dawn, things
    happen.
I got pulled out of bed, I wasn't done nappin'.
Didn't get to grieve my loss, I had to please my boss;
Get those trucks loaded and on the road.
All the while collecting interest on the debt I owed.

It was mounting; the cost was so enormous I stopped
    counting.
Tried to bury it with opiates.
The more I took, the more I'd forget what it must have
    been like for you that day.
I know you didn't really want to go away.
But you made a commitment,
You said you were going to kill yourself and you
    meant it.

NEEDLE BUDDIES

When life gets hard, no sunshine in sight,
Up my sleeve I have a card, helps me through the night.
The "ace" I speak of is better than Teletubbies,
She's my dearest friend, compadre, my needle buddy.
When we have dope and syringes galore,
We hide ourselves away, locked behind the door.

The lights get dim as we cook up our "smack"
She pushes the stem when we smoke crack.
Ecstasy pills make us all lovey-dovey.
Alone at last, just me and my needle buddy.
I fix the rig and play pogo stick
While she prays to the toilet, getting so sick.

These are the things we love to do;
Speedballin heroin, sharing needles with you,
When the junk hits our veins, eyes roll back.
"Save me a bump, give me that back."
Thinking of her always brings on a "chubby"
Can't wait to be alone again with my needle buddy.

SUCKER PUNCH

Cocaine is the Devil's candy. It will cause you to do things totally out of your character and go places you don't belong. It will make you pay more than you want to spend and keep you longer than you want to stay. It is a black hole, a vortex of evil that has only one purpose: destruction. It is a lie from the pits of hell and can only be overcome by the power of God. The depths of deprivation and lengths of lasciviousness are without parallel. Cocaine is a thief. It kisses you with loving affection and then it kicks you in the groin. It laughs at you when you cry. It rejoices when you suffer. Cocaine will gladly take all you have and then demand more. It is a bottomless pit, a dead end street, a dark alley, and an endless nightmare.

All of these descriptions are from my own first-hand experience. I was introduced to crack cocaine over fifteen years ago and I'm incarcerated right now because of it. I'm in a state-run correctional rehabilitation center in Bainbridge, GA. I've been locked up for 9 months and it is the longest period of time I've ever gone without experiencing the re-occurring bad dream of cocaine. These razor wire fences aren't keeping me in, they are keeping crack cocaine and all of its evil out. I'm 30 days away from my release. Cocaine is still out there and it wants me dead. Am I afraid? NO! For I can do all things through Christ who strengthens me. In Him I am more than a conqueror. But I also know that the Devil lurks about like a roaring lion seeking whomever he may devour. So what do I do? I move forward. I let go and let God. Step slow and steady. I take it one day at a time. I have blind faith because I now know that there is no temptation common to man but God is faithful to always make a way of escape. I can look back with confidence because even when cocaine had its grip on me, God was still faithful to rescue me from the snare of the fowler.

Allow me to take you back to one of my darker days. A day that was nearly my undoing. But by the grace of God, I escaped the plans of the Devil for my demise. I was working at a pizza place, a national chain, as a delivery driver. One of the cooks there had caught wind of my weakness for crack. He told me if I ever wanted some to come find him at the Augusta Hills Apartments. I resisted initially because, after all, I was and had been trying my best to quit doing it. I had a love/hate relationship with cocaine. It's called ambivalence. The very thing that attracted me also disgusted me. Such is the nature of crack. It is a paradox. It's confusing and it can't be explained. I was able to go for days, sometimes weeks without doing it, and then

I would be overcome with intense cravings and desire for it. I was powerless over it. I was subject to give in to the temptation, usually at the most unexpected times. There were times when I was able to postpone a relapse, but eventually, inevitably, I'd break and chase after it like a lost lover. It was like a light switch in my brain that would flip from "off" to "on" without warning. Once the switch turned to "on," I was at its mercy and could only delay the pending train wreck. I'd become nauseated and extremely anxious at the thought of using again because each episode was a game of Russian roulette. I'd never know how it was going to end, whom I'd end up with, or where I'd go to keep getting it. The term "one is too many and a thousand never enough" is custom-made for crack cocaine. I knew this all too well but could not manage to resist the "one" even though I knew it would set off a chain reaction like tumbling dominoes for the other "thousand."

Each ugly episode would hold the promise of being the last. This thought alone would play right into the desperateness of each relapse. I'd tell myself that this would be the last time I was going to do this, which would make me want to go to outrageous lengths to keep each relapse alive as long as possible. It is true insanity in every sense of the word. It would require divine intervention to bring each re-occurrence to an end. Cocaine has the power to motivate me to do desperate things and commit thorough harm. Once I give into the temptation, it's like Pandora's box being opened, unleashing an avalanche of poor judgment and erratic behavior. Sometimes the high would be so intense that I would ingest large amounts of benzodiazepines or alcohol in an attempt to slow down the rush. By itself, crack cocaine made me feel like I was strapped to the front of a run-away freight train plummeting from the edge of the earth with no way to stop it or get off. Another hit would turn the train into a Jacuzzi, but only for a moment. So I'd be stuck like chuck. Craving the relief of the warm Jacuzzi but perpetuating or shoveling coal into the boiler of the train. Like I said, it is insanity. When I'd combine alcohol and sedatives with it, there would be large gaps in consciousness where I was liable to do God only knows what.

Anyway, I was in the middle of one of these relapses and was trying to find Andre at the Augusta Hills Apartment Complex. Andre drove a primer-colored Cutlass with rims on it, a very easy car to spot. As I entered the parking lot, I was disappointed in not seeing his car. I circled around several times to look for him, but no luck. Everything within me screamed to just go home, but I was on a mission: I had to score. The craving for that "Jacuzzi" was in control even though I knew the freight train ride from hell would follow. On my second or third time around the complex, I saw four or five guys standing near one of the apartments. It was obvious to me that they were selling dope, so I cautiously decided to approach them. I used Andre as an icebreaker by asking if they had seen him.

"Andre who?" they snapped back. I didn't know his last name so I described his car instead. "Man, get your butt outta here!" one of them yelled. My short hair always made me look like the police and was a cause for suspicion. I pressed on by telling them it was OK and that I was "cool," all I wanted was a "dub" (slang for $20 worth of crack). They all backed away warily since they didn't know me, all but one. He told me to throw my money on the ground as he placed a piece of dope on the curb. This way he could make the sale without a hand-to-hand exchange. I dropped a twenty-dollar bill on the ground then walked over and grabbed the "dub" off the curb. Mission accomplished, I thought to myself. I drove to a secluded spot a few miles away and jumped feet first into the Jacuzzi. It felt good; it seemed to make sense for a moment. I actually felt like it brought me closer to God. Like I've said before, it is insanity. I was experiencing the affectionate kiss of cocaine. It is mind-numbing and it messes your soul. But it is counterfeit, a fake, and a liar. Crack cocaine feels like the Holy Spirit. It touches you deep down inside, it makes everything disappear; all pain, all worry, and all of your money.

God designed us to be sensitive to His Spirit. It can be felt through prayer and heartfelt worship, through living right and holy intentions, it comes from a purposeful effort, it can't be bought. The Devil has a counterfeit for everything God has and one of his imitations for the Holy Spirit is cocaine. God rewards effort and sincere desire with His presence. What He gives is eternal and has no negative side effects, but you have to put the work into it first. Satan offers buy now, pay later credit. A person can have the Jacuzzi experience for a $20 bill, but they're gonna ride that freight train too! Just like a sharp fishing hook can penetrate your flesh so smoothly, but when you try to remove it, the jagged barb on the other side snags and tears and refuses to be pulled out. I knew all of this to be true, but insanity has a clever way of clouding one's judgment.

So, my moment of bliss is quickly coming to an end and my front row seat on the train is fast approaching, in fact, I'm already strapped in. I'm left feeling as desperate as someone in a house fire. All exits are blocked, there seems to be no way out except to jump back into the Jacuzzi. Can you see where this is leading? One is too many and a thousand never enough. Insanity can be described as doing the same thing over and over but each time expecting different results. This is what crack does. It tells you to do just one more, that it will satisfy you so much that you won't need to do another one. This is the thought pattern of an insane person. The thing that is telling me I have to have one more, is also telling me that just one more will be enough. The Devil is a liar and crack cocaine is his candy. But it is too late, I've already tasted the first piece and more is all I want. With all the earnestness and passion of someone cashing in a million dollar lottery ticket, I leave my secluded spot and head back to Augusta Hills Apartments. The drive is excruciating. Operating a car at 35 MPH and negotiating traffic while feeling the freight train pounding in my heart and head is very difficult. I grip the steering wheel with sweaty palms and grit my teeth like I'm in the front row of a horror show matinee. My pupils are dilated from the cocaine and my stomach churns like I'm about to speak in public. Basically I'm desperate. I can't calm down and all I can think about is getting more. This is the kick in the groin after the affectionate kiss. This is when the devil laughs at you. I had fallen for the sweet taste of the candy and now I was stuck with the bitter aftertaste of desperation. It's one of the worst feelings in the world. All I can think about is the relief from the Jacuzzi and I'll go to any lengths to find it.

Eventually I arrive back at the apartments and turn into the parking lot. Again I don't see Andre's car, nor do I see the guys I bought from earlier. "Darn," I say to myself. The craving for more just gets worse and worse, so I decide to take matters into my own hands. Exiting my truck, I walk toward the apartment where the guys were earlier. There is a breezeway that divides the four apartments and I walk through it knocking on each door like some sort of cracked out Avon salesman. At first nobody responded to my knocking so I started to climb the stairs that led to the second floor. But before I could get halfway up the steps, I heard one of the downstairs doors pop open. Glancing down through the railing, I recognized the faces of the guys I had met earlier. I did a U-turn and galloped back down the steps while saying, "Oh, there you are. I thought you had left," like we were old friends from way back. But my little icebreaker was met with cold steel glares from all five of them. "How did you know we were in here?" growled one of them. They were already suspicious of me; now I had knocked on their door, a very uncool thing to do in the drug world. I knew this, but desperate people do stupid things. "I didn't know. I just figured you all might be in one of these apartments," I explained as I pulled out another $20 bill. "Can I get another dub?" I asked as they all filed out the door and surrounded me. I felt their mistrust and anger as I could tell they too were high and very paranoid. I tried to back away because I was feeling trapped and I just knew things were not going well. I managed to ease to my left, but the bushes that lined the front of the apartments hindered my progress.

That's when I noticed the largest one in the group slipping into my blind spot just behind my shoulder. I wanted to run... I wanted to score. I was stuck in no man's land. Then suddenly one of them held out a piece of crack in his hand and said, "Is this what you want?" I felt myself relax, letting down my guard long enough to lean forward and take a closer look at the object in his hand. Just when I thought everything was going to work… BOOM!! The hulking figure to my left sucker punched me with enough force to knock me out. I came to a few moments later, face down in the bushes. My face was bleeding from multiple scratches caused by the pruned branches in the hedgerow. It looked like someone dragged some coiled-up barbed wire across my face. I sprang to my feet with a rush of adrenaline and fear. "What was that for?" I demanded as I held my jaw. "Oh, you must want another one," said the big guy who decked me. Then they all closed in on me with their fists balled up and teeth clinched in anger. This is it, I thought to myself. I'm about to get my butt kicked. I'd been dancing with the Devil and now it was time to pay the piper. I braced myself for the attack and grimaced with dreadful anticipation.

Then, just as suddenly as I had been sucker punched I heard—"Wait. Don't hurt him, he's cool." I turned my head towards the parking lot to see Andre whipping in with his primed-out Cutlass. "Oh thank God." I sighed. My would-be assailants stopped dead in their tracks and unclenched their fists. Andre jumped out of his car, leaving the door open, and jogged over to where I was standing. He repeated his appeal for my release and said, "He's cool. I know him." His intervention had saved me in the nick of time. "Man, thanks 'Dre', I've been looking for you all day." I said with grateful relief. "Sure man, I got you, buddy. Now what you need?" he said as he put his arm around me. "Oh man, I don't know… you got a dub?"

CLASS

*Mike had been court ordered to attend a state-run reha-
bilitation center in Bainbridge, GA, for 6 months. The
following poems were written while he was in class.

This is how I get through class,
Scratching down poems while sitting on my butt.
Conversations wax and wane,
Becoming ever-increasing, excruciating pain.
Talking about children and how to raise them,
Should they be spanked or should we praise them?
It all really doesn't matter to me,
I'm just waiting for the day I'll go free!

Time stands still like a broken clock,
My butt is so numb it feels like a rock.
Can this really be happening today?
I want it to end, God hear me pray.
There has to be some reason to this rhyme,
Is this just punishment for my crime?

CLASS

Broad is the scope of every question.
Is there an end to the day's lesson?
It's really quite basic and not too deep.
The biggest challenge is not falling asleep.
I've managed to pass nearly an hour somehow,
The pain in my butt feels like I'm having a cow!!

Surely I'll find a way to get through this day
Once this class is over, I'll be on my way.

CLASS #2

Good morning glory—hallelujah to ya!
What is your story? And what's been going through ya?
I'm sittin in this class, in the CRA!
Only eight more weeks, and I'll go home to stay!

I'm movin'—Without a doubt.
I'm movin'—I'm getting out.
I'm movin'—I'm going far.
I'm movin'—Oh yes, we are.

This is a story about drug addiction.
I was saved by His glory.
I was spared from perdition.
He came down to me in my hour of need.
He sent His Holy Spirit to set my soul free.

What God Has Taught Me From Failure

The biggest lesson I learned from failure has probably been that life goes on even if I don't succeed at everything I try. This realization lets me know that tomorrow will come and bring with it a new chance to try again. "For His mercies are new each day." With God's help and what I learned from failure, I can adjust my strategy, rule out what didn't work, and reattempt whatever it is I'm trying to achieve.

Failure has also taught me to persevere and keep trying until I succeed. Failure has taught me humility. It has let me know that I'm not perfect, nor do I want to be. I've learned to depend on God and ask for His help in every situation. The process of being humbled is not fun to endure, but if I allow it to truly reduce my ego, the end result is pleasing to God. Failure has allowed me to enjoy success much more than if I had never failed.

I know the agony of defeat so well that the triumph of success is much sweeter. Failure has taught me to enjoy the times when situations do work out, knowing that every good and perfect gift comes from above. I learn more from failure and loss that I do from success. Pain and disappointment cause me to seek God and His answers.

What Has God Taught Me From Lack Of Money?

Being short on finances has been a wonderful way for God to demonstrate His love for me. Lack of money had made me truly appreciative of the things in life that are either free or can't be bought. Some of the free things include: laughter, sunsets, sunrises, friends and family, a kiss from my wife, a playful game of fetch with my dog, walking in the woods or along the edge of the beach. The list is endless for me.

But I only became aware of how much there is to be had for free because there was a lack of money. I've also learned to appreciate all the things I have that can't be bought, no matter how much money I may have. Things like my health, my salvation, my freedom, and the joy I feel from knowing Jesus.

Money can be a distraction from the things in life that matter most. It can blind you into thinking that material possessions are what make you happy. Some of my most precious memories are from moments that came while not having any money to speak of. Freedom is just a word for nothing left to lose. Once I understood what was truly valuable, I never became discouraged from my lack of money.

BETWEEN

What will happen remains to be seen.
Where will I go on those days in-between?
The here and now drifts idly by,
Anxiously waiting for my chance to fly
Out that gate to the ones I love,
Reaching upward for the skies above.
Far beyond all I could imagine or think,
Pushing my limits beyond the brink.

A chance to express myself in all I do,
A chance to show my love felt for you.
I want to pray for His will be done.
I want to trust Holy Spirit, Father, and Son.
Take my life and make it shine
A light in the darkness, no longer blind.
Eyes wide open, perceiving all around
Divinely woven, no longer bound.

BETWEEN

A sense of joy bubbling up inside me
Like a child with a toy, playing free,
Out in the yard, no limits or debts.
Sincere regard, engines roaring, firing jets.
Can you hear me? Don't want to scream.
Will you cheer me on these days between?

HIGH RISK SITUATION

*Most relapses occur because the recovering person does not adequately plan for potential high-risk situations or they have not learned effective coping strategies to handle high-risk situations without using alcohol and other drugs.

It's a high-risk situation,
One God under one nation.
Criminal thinking addiction
Passing down the conviction.
Elements of surprise, like blinded eyes,
When will I realize—all of these tears I've cried –
All the fears I've tried—all access denied.
Emotional pain, it's all the same, I can't refrain
It's a run a way train, going down the drain, so hard to
    explain.
There are no rules to this game, it's insane.
What's its name? It's called addiction.

So come and get some, it will ruin you,
It will run you through,
What you gonna do?

HIGH RISK SITUATION

It's twenty-four seven like seventh heaven, a masquerade
   party,
Addicted are we: life in the gutter, like no other, its
   there to poison you.
To make you puke, rearrange what you do, it will
   handle you.
Incarceration, segregation, frustration, I want to kill
   you all,
Up against the wall, watch you fall, disembowel you as
   you crawl.

Close your eyes, like circling flies, help me realize all
   the days I've lied.
Crawling on the floor like a filthy whore,
Locked behind the door, scraping knees, help me please.
I don't want these infirmities; I need a strategy from
   depravity, alone with me.
Why won't you leave me be?
Blinded eyes, I cannot see through the trees.
Please help me get rid of these inconsistencies.

It's upon me now, I've found it somehow, and my hands
   are on the plow.
Fields of wheat, back on my feet, I think it's neat.
Pull apart the sheets in the bed I lie, no longer asking
   why.
On the mountain high, can't deny the love from the sky.
The Son is here drawing me near, erasing my fear.

PRISON VISION

Panting like the deer, water flows, no one knows where
it goes or the details it shows.
They're tiny, like glitter on the ground, reflective and
shiny,
Scattered about in every direction, misguided and lying
full of deception.
It's a fallacy out to hurt me, punch me in the nose, like
a drug overdose.

Unconscious and dying, took too many of the pills I
was buying.
It's got the doctor shaking his head and sighing, undi-
agnosed, looking gross,
Borderline comatose.
Puking up charcoal, liquid and black, see it out of your
mouth flow.
Did it save your life?
Put an end to your strife?
Or did it cut you like a knife?
Lift you hopeless and abandoned—fell slap off the
wagon.
Run over by a movin' train you were tagin',
Spray paint expressing the hate, leaving your mark so
they'd appreciate
The pain you were feeling, sick of the cards they were
dealing.
A run-down casino, thought you would feel no more
pain, it's a shame.

HIGH RISK SITUATION

A rigged-up game—backside of Vegas—like the sign
    that said "Don't trespass."
It all happened so fast, you were outta gas, wanted to
    have the last laugh,
It wasn't funny, it was disgusting.

NO ONE

No one can tell me that I'm feeling bad today. Nobody can steal my joy, my victory. I've come too far, through too much to even entertain a negative idea. It's the small foxes that ruin the vine. The little comments that seep from open sewers solely designed to defile and detour. "Oh look, a blood drive bus." "I ain't giving blood unless they pay me!" "You know as a convicted felon, you can't possess a firearm." "I'm gonna break the law anyway. I'm gonna carry my heater."

I come against the negative mind; I know from where it is born. The author of lies and discord burps his filth into the air like a sulfur smokestack from the seventies. Raw pollution, no filter, no qualities of purity. I put on the gas mask of His word and refuse to inhale the toxic waste of pessimism and unbelief.

Lord, You are the way, the truth and the life—You give life and life more abundant. You are Alpha and Omega. Amen

HOLD ON

Addiction let go of me!! This is the way it has to be?
My Savior has set me free. You no longer have a hold
    on me.
My future is all I see, I'm claiming my destiny,
Maximizing my ability, nobody rides for free,
Nobody gets it like they want it to be.
Everybody walks on by like they're safe or something.

Oh no, no—nobody, nobody has a hold on me.
I'm standing up accepting my responsibility,
This is the way I want it to be.
A gift from God—finally free.
Blind eyes have opened, I like what I see.
Addiction has lost its hold on me.

ONE THOUSAND
DREAMS

Over and over they occur it seems,
Images and visions from a thousand dreams.
Waking up wet with sweat,
Paralyzed and traumatized, unable to scream.
Questions and answers entangled,
Murky hallucinations jumbled up, mangled.
Home in the darkness, strangers I cannot see.
Prophetic encounters, what are they saying to me?
Burn out my brain, burn throughout the night,
Tears on my pillow, stained, clutching covers tight.
Always looking back, such crazy nights
Virtual heart attack, no end in sight.
Is this an attempt to bring me down?
Nighttime images swirling around.
It's not every night I'm cursed with second sight.
But on the days it's there, I get quite a scare,
Enough to climb tall mountains—leap!
Just stay calm, here comes the dawn
Awaiting my wake from this sleep.

ABOUT TO ROCK

For those about to rock, I rebuke you.
For those about to rock, I don't salute you.
You steal my life, anti-creator,
You get under my skin, won't see you later.
Livin' a lie, don't want to debate it,
Won't pick you up again.

Come on over here, boy, I'll make you fly high.
Won't show you no respect.
Call the name of the game.
They call it ridin' the Lady Train.
Everybody else is just green.
It will become a monster,
A nightmare without a scream.

Don't come here no more,
'Cause you're a cruel criminal,
A poor boy won't show you no sympathy.
Mama just relapsed again.

PRISON VISION

I put a gun against my head.
Didn't mean to make you cry,
It sends shivers down my spine.
Makes me wish I'd never been born at all.

Don't want to live with this ghost,
Want to serve the One I desire most.
I am still dreaming of Your face,
Just want to bask in some Son shine.

GIVE

Do I have anything to offer?
Does anybody need me?
Can this make a difference?
Will there be a happy ending?
Is the message worth writing?
Is it worth sending?
Unknown faces staring back at me.
Do I possess the answer?
Do I possess the key?
Can I feel it with sympathy?
Can it be orchestrated?
Put together like a symphony?

Number one with a bullet
Chart-topping bestseller.
Am I just full of it?
Will I be able to tell her?
Waiting for tomorrow to find it,
A mountain so tall.
Am I afraid to climb it?
All I can give is my all.

PRISON VISION

Does that satisfy the desire?
Will it answer the call?
Growing everyday higher
Am I just afraid to fall?

A PRAYER

Father,

I always thought prison walls were impenetrable for me, a place reserved for society's worst and most deserving criminals, but prison is no respecter of persons. It is a cold, lifeless structure, built to contain, restrain, and obtain the vilest creature on Earth, the human being. My sins against man were small, just enough to qualify me for this place, yet I know in my heart that I was guilty of the worst crime possible, the re-crucifixion of Christ each time I transgressed from His goodness to the company of fools and demons. Deserving to be struck down, cast out, uprooted, I lingered on the edge of destruction for years. Praise God, though, He looked into my heart, bypassed my flesh to see a man trapped within a curse from the Destroyer. He saw pain and guilt rather than causal arrogance and thus has been oh so merciful even during this time of scourging!!

Jesus, You really are a friend of sinners and One much acquainted with sorrow!! Thank You for this—my Lord—my Savior! Amen

EVERYBODY'S INN

Is everybody in?
I'm not sure where to start.
How do I begin to begin?
It's a matter of the heart.
This condition of original sin,
A hotel built for you and me.
No down payment required,
We're born into it; cost is free.

Sticky clay in which we're mired,
No way out, within our ability.
Satan's prearranged the stay,
Have plenty of rooms, always a vacancy.
We may not have bought it,
But there is a high price to pay,
No matter which one we commit
The list is as long as the day.
Whether in part or in bit,
Imperfection is the only way,

EVERYBODY'S INN

Qualifies us for the gates of hell
Ever since Adam fell.
Is this the way it has to be?
I wish there were a better way.
Does this have to be our fate?
Jesus, will You hear me pray?
I need You now, the hour is late.
Holy Spirit come, never go away.

JUST FOR TODAY

Something deep inside me wants to scream!!
Will I actually live out these dreams?
Never deliver myself over.
Life slipping past, growing older.
Spring rushing forward fast, winter of discontent ever
    colder.
But now I stand alone, I want to let You know,
I've found a reason to come boldly before Your throne.
Now, just time on my hands, I'm not the one to argue.
This is my destined season, orchestrated, prearranged,
All by You!

Life's been good to me; it's been good to me so far.
Couldn't ask for more, no need to wish upon a star.
I'll keep on going, faith and hope rushing forward.
These are my thoughts, I pray.
They are enough, just for today!

EMPTY

Well she cries and she cries
All night to the sound of the freeway hum.
And she swears and she swears
She'll be gone when the daylight comes.
But she's so scared, she's so scared
To return to where she comes from.
As the sun starts to rise
There remain the tearstains in her eyes
Watching her life slowly pass her by.

So she cries and she cries
Over the beast that refuses to die.
It's her arm that keeps her broke
And the fire she has to stoke.
Brings the night back around,
Puts her down on the ground.
Unable to leave this filthy town.
Oh, how she wants to go
But there's a train, riding slow
Won't pick her up 'til the next go 'round.

PRISON VISION

So she sighs and she sighs
All her life she's lost and never found.
And this train is filled with pain
From the memories that remain.
Searching high and low
Till the morning starts to glow.
Shining light upon the stain,
Plunging deep to fill her vein.

OUR FATHER

Our Father who art in heaven, allow me to know Your
    name,
Let Your will be made clear, shine Your light, remove
    my shame.
Give me Your way each and every day,
This is what I want to preach and say.
I can't wait to see Your face,
To feel Your love, to feel Your embrace.
For the times I've known it,
But didn't talk too much about it.
Forgive me, Lord, for living like a refugee.
For allowing myself to be set adrift,
Floating aimlessly in an endless sea.
Any part in the storm was my excuse to set sail,
Living outside the norm, knocking on the gates of hell.
You've placed me back on solid ground,
I can see Your grace each time I look around.
Let me not be tempted to fall,
I give these cares to You, You can have them all.
Thank you, Jesus, for what You've done,
I submit this prayer to You, Father, Holy Ghost, and
    precious Son.

DREAMS

Late at night, drifting through my head
Dreams like sand shifting,
Filter my mind, find me in bed.
Recollections at dawn
Can't remember exactly what went on.
Images and visions mangled together,
Openings like deep incisions,
Rainless clouds, stormy weather.
Snapshots frozen in time.
Windows left open,
Is there a reason, is there a rhyme?

Subconscious films without a script,
Are they flashbacks from all the acid I've tripped?
Disasters and triumphs,
Simultaneous stories and plots,
Meaningless episodes twisted
Vortex of color, glossy snapshots.

They pick and choose the actors
It's impossible to add up all the factors.
But I still enjoy these dreams, as into my head they creep,
Finding me in bed alone as I sleep.

CLIMB

This feeling inside,
Slowly becoming my all in all.
Searching for a place to hide
Making me want to climb the walls.
Swimming around, restless pursuit,
Scratching my head, what should I do?

Urges and cravings, sometimes severe,
Spending my savings, drawing me near.
I'm growing closer, days are few
Looking over my shoulder,
Rearview mirror, same old view.
The open road lies ahead,
Winding snake, skin ready to shed.
Trapped in this body, can't escape,
Nerves are shoddy, can you relate?

I'm ready to scream, cry, sleep,
Will it leave if I try? Am I in too deep?
Dreaming about California, a quest headed west.
The sun it will warm ya. Will it be for my best?
Rules are meant to conform ya, Will I pass this test?

ANY THANG GOES

It's a simple case of anythang goes.
It's all senses erased with powder up the nose.
It's needles and rigs, those who were crumb snatchers
And those who were making it big, stuck in this shed.
Razor wire on the fence, tin roof over my head.
Constantly smelling the stench,
War stories and drug romance,
I just want it to end.
I'll leave when given the chance,
Find myself some new friends.

I've had enough of the endless tales,
Ecstasy pills, meth lab sales,
The times they did so much—it can't be true
Not for a minute.
I'm sick of details about drug use,
It's their lie and I don't want to be in it.
This is where drugs get ya,
Locked up with thugs, no way out.
I must refrain from relapse,
Is there any reason to doubt?

OXYCONTIN BLUES

Oxycontin will make us rotten, itching and scratching
    all day.
We put off our bills in exchange for these pills,
Despite how tiny they are.
In exchange for the need to relieve those pains,
We could almost afford a new car!
They're oh so great when for breakfast they're ate,
Two or three at a time.
But don't hesitate or wait too late
Once we've crossed that line.
They'll all be gone before too long—
Desperately needin' more.
We call all around; go out driving the town,
Anxiously searching to "score."
Finding none, we come undone,
Wind up flat on the floor.
So take my advice, don't think twice,
Consume this drug no more.
It costs all our money and it ain't even funny
When bubble gum we can't buy from a store.

IN-BETWEEN JAIL TIMES—
APRIL 2009 –
DECEMBER 2010

TRIED

I woke today, like any other, except a voice was in my
  head.
It said, "Seize this day, hug your mother, make a new
  friend,
A lovely lover, try to live again, respect a brother."
It's got me thinking; one more time around might do it.
One more time around might make it the day I tried.

So I swore this day to steal a thousand beggars' change
And give it to the rich.
But something came away and hit me with a switch.
Got me feeling phony, false teeth and wigs.
Like I'm rolling in blood and mud with all the other
  pigs.
One more time around might make it.
One more time around might take it.
The day I tried to live.

Now things aren't the same.
The game has changed and run away.
Like lepers' crutches on a holiday.

173

PRISON VISION

But I'm still thinkin' what might do it, might make it
    stay?
How much should I give?
Or should I even raise the shade?
The day I tried... to live.

HOSANNA

Lord, thank you for hearing my prayer.
It feels so good to know You are there.
No matter what may happen or come my way,
I know for sure You hear what I say.
Some things are big and some so small.
I thank You for the attention You give to them all.
So with that in mind, I make my request.
Steady and prepare my heart to receive Your best.

Help my life be a light unto You.
Praising You daily for all that You do.
Can I offer myself a sacrifice to Thee?
A sweet-smelling aroma is my plea.
I know without a doubt that You are alive
Walking next to me with each step that I stride.
Keep me from running too far ahead
Away from the sin and things that are dead.
I wish to be a pleasant surprise,
Like the moonshine at night and a morning's sunrise.
You are the light, the truth, and the way,
Live in my heart and forever there stay.

PRISON VISION

I release this request up to Your throne,
Knowing for sure with You I'm never alone.
You've saved my soul for all eternity,
Entering my heart while on bended knee,
Erasing my fault and washing me clean,
Showing me things never before seen.
Your face I will ever adore,
For You placed my sin on the ocean floor.

TIME

Days spent between here and there,
Hard to find new ways to express
All that I love, all that I care.
It's times like these that I've had to learn to live again.
Times like these I've learned to love again.
Now I say, "Hold on, hold on loosely,
But don't let go."
I'll find a new way to live,
A new way to let it show.

My best shot, give it all I've got,
I'll continue to try these times,
Writing on pages, scribbling down rhymes.
Lord, I'm amazed at all You do.
Amazed at all You've brought me through.
You've used these times, time and time again,
To show me Your mercy,
Always there, closer than a friend.

Now it's time to turn and face the change,
Though it is fascinating,
It still seems strange.

PRISON VISION

Yet it is times like these
I've learned to love again.
Times like these I've learned to live
Time and time again

GEORGIA,
FLOYD COUNTY JAIL–
DECEMBER 2010 – MAY 2011

MIND GAME

I'm trying to wrap my mind around this particular
stretch of time.
Struggling with these days that are this life of mine.
The nights aren't so bad, as a quiet fills the dorm.
But they seem to pass too fast, like the calm before the
storm.

On my bed I pray for God to see me through.
With steel doors locked tight, there is little else to do.
I long to feel the rush like the ones who go home.
But through empty halls of time, my thoughts are
forced to roam.

Still I know that I am so blessed, so I send praises to
the Lord.
The things that put me in this mess, I know I can't
afford.
Knowing that I'll leave this place behind with all its
shame,
I'll raise my hands in victory, as my mind wins the
game!

MOTHER'S NOTE

Mike was released from jail on May 20, 2011, and raised his hands in victory as God called him home on May 26, 2011. Drugs are a terrible thing and I pray that all of you who read his words will understand and heed his warning. God bless each one of you.

—Mike's mother

CPSIA information can be obtained at www.ICGtesting.com
Printed in the USA
LVOW040013240113

316990LV00001B/25/P